'I love this book! It has r   ly with
new passion. It will give   rt fresh
hope, fresh faith and fresh courage. ...   .urch to
work with him – rewriting the history of individuals, communities
and nations. But in the West the Church has become increasingly
irrelevant. The burning question is, "How can we become what God
originally intended us to be?" Scripture, church history, the current
worldwide work of God and John's long experience of church
leadership contain vital answers. Everyone has a part to play. Here's
your chance to fully play yours.'
Revd Canon John Coles, former leader of New Wine England

'As the age of Christendom closes, John McGinley doesn't believe
that further decline and cultural irrelevance are inevitable. Instead,
he anticipates a new reformation, urging followers of Jesus and
church leaders to recover a fresh vision of church. Laced with
helpful quotes, all eight chapters of *The Church of Tomorrow*
describe a key mark of the future Church, with each ending with a
powerful "personal response". This is a timely and prophetic book,
and should be read by all concerned not just that God's future
Church has a mission, but also that God's future mission has a
Church.'
Revd Dr Matthew Porter, author and vicar of St Michael le Belfrey
Church, York

'This vital book is a clarion call in a time where we as individual
followers of Jesus and the Church as a whole have a choice to
make. It is hard to ignore the case John so powerfully makes to get
ourselves ready for the pivotal season we are entering. Not only will
this book sharpen your mind and stir your heart, it gives space for
prayerful reflection and hugely practical steps to help us put what
God is saying to us into action. Thank you, John!'
Sarah Belcher, leader of Kingdom Embassy Church

'Are you ready for change? We have entered a new era and how we "do" church needs a radical overhaul if we are to see the nations transformed by the power of God. John writes in a way that equips the Church to "be" the Church through understanding the shifts that are happening and then challenging us to respond in a faith-filled, uncompromising way. I believe if we can take this to heart and get to our knees, we could be part of seeing a great global harvest in our lifetime.'

Anne Calver, author and overseer of Unleashed Church

'There was a deep ache in my heart as I read *The Church of Tomorrow*, but it was a pain accompanied by a louder song of hope. The ache was a profound longing for the renewal we are desperate to see, but this book is far from a lament of the current situation. It is bursting with crystal clarity, inspirational hope, biblical wisdom and evocative storytelling, leaving me with no doubt that not only is change possible, but here is the encouragement we need to get there. John is the real deal. *The Church of Tomorrow* is soaked in the wisdom, lived-out experience and prophetic imagination of its author. I pray that it leads to explosive growth and creativity in the Church and many coming to faith in Jesus.'

Phil Knox, author and head of mission to young adults at the Evangelical Alliance

'This is a book I wish I had written! John has done a superb job in bringing together biblical, historical, ecclesial and prophetic insights and voices to help us glimpse something of the heart and power of the Church of tomorrow. From the unshakeable starting-point confession and framework for our lives that "Jesus is Lord", to wonderful revelations about discipleship and the Church as a self-propagating, Spirit-led, planting community, John paints a hope-filled but challenging picture of this Church. The Church as a creative minority, no longer at the centre of culture, but on the margins of it is poised to have its greatest impact for 500 years. Read on and be inspired. Let's be the Church of tomorrow!'

Dr Nic Harding, author, director of the Kairos Connexion and Together for the Harvest, and founding pastor of Frontline Church

'Reading *The Church of Tomorrow* filled me with fresh vision and hope for the future of the bride of Christ. Drawing on teaching from Scripture, lessons from history and a prophetic sense of what the Spirit is saying to the Western Church today, John McGinley presents a compelling diagnosis of the Church's current condition and gives an insightful, creative, much-needed prescription for renewed life and energy for the body of Christ.'

Becky Harcourt, part of the leadership team of All Saints Woodford Wells and New Wine

'John describes this book as an invitation to hold the plumb line of Scripture, the Church in revival in history and the rapidly growing Church around the world up against the Church that you and I belong to in the West and to note the differences. And if that sounds as though it could only generate a troubling conclusion, then don't worry: yes, this book is honest and real, but it's also a hope-filled and inspiring read. This book is shot through with prayer and testimony. It will stretch your mind, warm your heart and feed your soul.'

Revd Canon John Dunnett, director of Strategy and Operations, The Church of England Evangelical Council

'These truly are significant times of reforming both in and outside the Church. I am so encouraged by what John has written in *The Church of Tomorrow*. The message is prophetic, practical and filled with promise for a better future. The reader will understand "why" we must change but is also given the "how". I highly recommend this book.'

Steve Uppal, senior leader, All Nations Church

'I was on my knees in repentance and prayer within 15 minutes of reading this book. It is dynamite. John's ability to express how we have lost our way as the people of God and the years of displacement from truth and demonstrations of the power of God struck me deeply. Yet, pages later, tears wiped, hope had arisen. Hope for the emergence and wildness of a vastly improved Church, hope for our moving in God-given momentum. I wanted to run to the altar and cry afresh for God to move through us, for our lives to become the story he wants told on the earth today. This is the day of a surge of the power of God in, on and through his people. He is ending our separation from fruitfulness, for we have hit demonstration season in the kingdom, where we like Paul will not preach the gospel with wise words, but with demonstrations of the Spirit's power. John continually amazes me. I love watching how he does life; he is a wondrous mix of apostolic strategy and deep tenderness, of ability to action and pioneer yet with total dependence on the flow of the Holy Spirit. He is a giant among men and we are all richer for having a window into his world and writings. Let this book transform you; come to it with your heart open to the possibilities of what you could be if God wrestled you into the heart of his will.'
Emma Stark, director of Global Prophetic Alliance

'A masterful manifesto for missional church, simply identifying the "Signs of the Times" and exploring both the biblical means and methods already pointing to the breakthroughs we need. A must-read for anyone in church, lay and ordained, who recognizes the current challenges of moving into recently uncharted landscapes and is looking for a compass. John combines incisive honesty in analysing the radical challenges of our changed context with a disarming combination of loving sensitivity and merciful understanding. John has a proven track record of outstanding missional leadership in both Hinkley and multicultural Leicester. He brings all this experience to bear on the kingdom needs of our

very challenging contexts. A must-read for lay and ordained leaders across the board. The best toolkit for this to become the "Church of Today"!'
Bob and Mary Hopkins, leaders of Anglican Church Planting Initiatives

'*The Church of Tomorrow* is a prophetic acclamation, calling the body of Christ to dream again! John perfectly addresses the defaults and traditions that have kept our churches stuck in the twenty-first century, inviting us into God's heart for a "new thing". John provides fresh revelation and practical insight into the cultural infrastructure needed to steward a new move of God in our churches, like multiplication and creativity. Those reading this book will experience fresh hope, faith and imagination for their church communities as the Holy Spirit reveals what's possible for the Church.'
Revd Wole Agbaje, senior pastor, Imprint Church

'In this book, John sets out a big vision of what church could and should look like. He challenges us about our priorities and our procedures. He encourages us with reminders of all the ways in which God is at work in our world. And perhaps most importantly he asks us big questions about what we might need to do in the present in order that we can step forward into the Church of tomorrow.'
Revd Kate Wharton, vicar of St Bartholomew's Church, Roby, Liverpool

THE CHURCH OF
TOMORROW

John McGinley works for the Gregory Centre for Church Multiplication (CCX) as Executive Director of Myriad. They have a vision to serve the planting of thousands of new churches as part of the Mixed Ecology vision and strategy of the Church of England and to inspire such growth across the whole of God's Church in the UK. John has 25 years' experience of church leadership, planting churches and leading missional communities. He has been involved in training and mentoring leaders across the UK as part of his national role with New Wine, and internationally he is involved in discipleship and church-planting training in 20 nations. His previous books *Mission-Shaped Grace* and *Mission Shaped Living* reflect his passion to restore making disciples to the centre of our understanding of church and discipleship. He is married to Bridget, and they have two grown-up daughters.

THE CHURCH OF TOMORROW

Being a Christ-centred people
in a changing world

John McGinley

First published in Great Britain in 2023

Society for Promoting Christian Knowledge
36 Causton Street
London SW1P 4ST
www.spck.org.uk

Copyright © John McGinley 2023

All rights reserved. No part of this book may be reproduced or transmitted in
any form or by any means, electronic or mechanical, including photocopying,
recording, or by any information storage and retrieval system, without permission
in writing from the publisher.

SPCK does not necessarily endorse the individual views contained
in its publications.

Unless otherwise noted, Scripture quotations are taken from The Holy Bible,
New International Version (Anglicized edition), copyright © 1979, 1984, 2011
by Biblica. Used by permission of Hodder & Stoughton Ltd, an Hachette UK
company. All rights reserved. 'NIV' is a registered trademark of Biblica. UK
trademark number 1448790.

Scripture quotations marked 'KJV' are taken from The Authorized (King James) Version.
Rights in the Authorized Version in the United Kingdom are vested in the Crown.
Reproduced by permission of the Crown's patentee, Cambridge University Press

A Grief Observed by CS Lewis © copyright 1961 CS Lewis Pte Ltd (rest of world,
excluding UK) and © Faber and Faber Ltd (UK)
Mere Christianity by CS Lewis © copyright 1942, 1943, 1944, 1952 CS Lewis Pte Ltd
The Screwtape Letters by CS Lewis © copyright 1942 CS Lewis Pte Ltd
Extracts reprinted by permission

British Library Cataloguing-in-Publication Data
A catalogue record for this book is available from the British Library

ISBN 978-0-281-08638-2
eBook ISBN 978-0-281-08639-9
Audiobook ISBN 978-0-281-08748-8

1 3 5 7 9 10 8 6 4 2

Typeset by Fakenham Prepress Solutions, Fakenham, Norfolk NR21 8NL
First printed in Great Britain by Clays Ltd
Subsequently digitally printed in Great Britain

eBook by Fakenham Prepress Solutions, Fakenham, Norfolk NR21 8NL

Produced on paper from sustainable forests

To my parents Jack and Ruth, who were the first to teach me to make Jesus Lord of my life. I am forever grateful.

Acknowledgements

There are no solitary authors; it is always a community that writes a book and I am grateful for the community of people who have encircled me as I have written *The Church of Tomorrow*. First, this book would be very thin if it weren't for the saints living and dead who have mentored me through their writings, lives and example. One of the visions for this book was to make their wisdom available to you as you navigate these uncertain times.

I am grateful for the team at SPCK Publishing and especially my editor Elizabeth Neep. Your reading experience is vastly improved because of her gracious, clear and wise guidance.

My colleagues at the Gregory Centre for Church Planting constantly inspire me. It is a privilege to be part of a team of people who are ambitious for God's kingdom and humble and generous as we share the adventure of joining in with the Holy Spirit as he renews his Church.

The church planters whom I meet through my Myriad work are my heroes. This book is because of them. I pray that something of what I have written will open doors and clear space for more of you to emerge and more churches to be planted.

I am grateful to all those who have read the drafts of this book and given feedback and made corrections: Catherine Ellerby, Lorraine Wright, Alice Bruce, David Vincent and Cathy Deng.

And most of all, thank you to my wife Bridget. I couldn't have written this without your love and support in giving me time to write this book and helping me in the moments when it seemed an impossible task. Thank you.

Foreword

We are living in a time of extraordinary change and uncertainty about the future. And this experience is not just in our wider society; it is a living reality for Christians and local churches everywhere. In *The Church of Tomorrow*, John McGinley invites us to engage with God, his word and the worldwide Church, and to look for the pathways and pictures the Spirit has provided to help us in times such as these. I have the privilege of working with John at the Gregory Centre for Church Multiplication, and he always encourages us to seek what God is saying and doing. It is a welcome and challenging invitation, and I am so grateful for his friendship and to have him on the team.

This is a hopeful book, in which the possibility of new life and renewal is described with passion, informed by voices from across the world and church history. It is a practical book, as spiritual disciplines and missionary practices are described, and we are invited to respond personally. It is also a prophetic book, as John challenges us with the need for new patterns and pathways to navigate the territory we find ourselves in today. I anticipate that you won't agree with everything you read here, but that's not the aim. What John has written is a firm prompt that stimulates a response and encourages us to engage with this cultural moment, prayerfully and in conversation with others, to discern what the Spirit might be saying to the Church.

As the Bishop of Islington, with responsibility for church planting, I am privileged to see the wonderful creativity, faith and diversity of the Church and to see so many different forms of church beginning to emerge and work together in partnership. I have seen this personally in Imprint Church, planted in the City of London, exploring its workplace context with huge creativity around performing arts; in WAVE Church, enabling people with and without learning disabilities to worship with singing, Makaton signing and creative teaching; and in the reopened and rejuvenated parish church of St Michael's Fulwell. The creator Spirit is bringing many new things to birth, and it is exciting to behold.

There is a sense within all of this that we are being invited by God to be ecclesiologists, who think deeply about the nature of church, and how we can fulfil the call of God to join him in his mission to reconcile the world to himself. The question 'what is church?' is a live one. As we wrestle with this, it is vital that we don't polarize different traditions or set old and new forms of church against each other, but rather that we begin to see the riches God has deposited in every form of church. We need them all. Within the Church of England, Mixed Ecology is a phrase that is gaining traction in giving people a picture of how this might look. Just as in a garden, where each variety of plant grows best in particular places and soils, God enables different forms of church to thrive in different communities, fulfilling different aspects of his mission, and yet all united in him.

John describes the place we find ourselves in today – one that some commentators describe as the time between Christendom and so-called post-Christendom – as 'the conflicted middle'. In Joshua 3, we find the Israelites camped on the banks of the River Jordan being told that they will enter the unfamiliar territory of Canaan the next day. God opens a pathway through the sea, but before the river parts he asks his people to do two things: to consecrate themselves afresh to him, and for the priests to step out into the water.

The Church of Jesus Christ belongs to God, and it is the presence and work of the Holy Spirit that forms us as he unites his people in Christ. Whatever each of us is called to do personally, a clear call that comes from this book is the need for a deeper consecration to and dependency on God. And as we do this, we wait for the first step into the future that God calls us to take. It won't necessarily be clear, and there is no guarantee of success, but that is the life of discipleship: to put our hand in God's and step forward with him.

As well as engaging with the big picture of all this, my prayer is that *The Church of Tomorrow* will equip you to discern what God is calling you to do in your own context and strengthen you to take that next step.

The Rt Revd Dr Ric Thorpe, Bishop of Islington and director of the Gregory Centre for Church Multiplication

Contents

Introduction

Christ is the Lord of a history that moves. He not only holds the beginning and the end in his hands, but he is in history with us, walking ahead of us to where we are going.

—Thomas Merton[1]

I saw a large crowd of people working hard on a massive wooden structure. They gathered to pray but nothing happened, they went off again and made more pieces to add to it. This same sad scene went on for some time, but no matter how hard they worked, nothing happened. Soon, I began to hear a sound; it was distant at first, but it grew louder and louder. Then I saw it, a massive body of people – of every age and nationality – came running, dancing and shouting, shapeless like a flood.

I heard them say, 'He makes all things new!' as they smashed through the man-made structure, which fell with a great crash! Those who had been building responded in different ways. Some fell to the ground in despair in the midst of the rubble. Others began to fight with the new crowd, trying to make them stop. Still others grabbed armfuls of what had collapsed and went off and tried to rebuild what had fallen. One last group just left the rubble and joined the dance with joy!

I felt the Lord speak: 'I will not bless that which is born of the arm of the flesh. This new move will be shapeless, yet structured like a mighty flood, unstoppable and alive! Like the flames in a fire, my people will dance the dance of the redeemed across the nations. In the midst of apparent desolation, a new thing shall be born, the old man-made structures shall come crashing to the ground, but my faith-filled bride shall arise dancing out of the ashes.' It is time to join the dance!

This is a prophetic word given to the Church in the UK recently, which I will come back to later. It presents a challenging but beautiful picture of God doing a new thing. I wonder what response it prompts in you?

All the way through its 2,000-year history the Church has developed and changed as it has crossed into new cultures and faced different challenges. We can describe this general change as evolution. But at certain times, roughly every 500 years (more about this later too), the Church experiences something more like a revolution, where God turns everything that we have become familiar with upside down. These are the moments of reformation that we can recognize in the Church's history. But history also teaches us that these seasons are difficult to discern and to navigate for those of God's people who are caught in the midst of them. And, as I pray and work with hundreds of churches and leaders across the country, I sense that we find ourselves in such a time today. This book is written to help you prepare for this; even more than that, to enable you to embrace and join in with it because you have a part to play in shaping the Church of tomorrow.

The heart behind this book is one of love and compassion for the Church and the faithful followers of Jesus who are beginning to ask, 'Why isn't it working any more?' And let's be really honest, for many of us it isn't working. The Church in the Global South is growing rapidly and yet closer to home we are experiencing decline, bringing great sadness, disappointment and anxiety about the future. And Jesus shares our grief and brokenness as he prays for us. As the third-century church father Origen wrote: 'If Jesus wept over Jerusalem, he has much more reason to weep over the church.' But Jesus not only weeps with us, he also calls us to rise and follow him.

My prayer is that this book might contribute to the wake-up call God is delivering to his Church. This call is merciful and gracious, but it is also holy and fierce as Jesus wants his Church back and is saying, as he did to Pharaoh many centuries ago, 'Let my people go.' This work of liberation is what we call reformation.

Why does God do this? Following Jesus involves shared patterns and practices that enable people to form church communities. These church traditions have enabled people to live out their faith in different generations and contexts. They are the channels through which Jesus' life-giving presence flows in our lives. But human beings have a tendency to institutionalize these patterns and traditions. We end up focusing on the trellis that helps the plant to grow instead of the plant, and over time that trellis becomes the bars of a prison cell which traps and restricts the life of the Church. Instead of being a growing plant crying out for support and structure, we become a structure desperately crying out for life and growth.

Bishop Mark Dyer suggests that every 500 years or so the Church is compelled to hold a 'rummage sale'[2] in which the things that have served us in the past but are now cluttering up the Church are thrown out. Bob Mumford conducts a similar analysis in *Stepping Over the Threshold*, where he writes about our current situation saying, 'I am deeply convicted that this present threshold is the transition out of a 500-year season in Church history.'[3] He describes how since its birth the Church has gone through a major and often convulsive transition approximately every 500 years and that this was often mirrored by the surrounding society. His analysis moves from Pentecost to AD 480 where the fall of the Roman Empire releases the Church into a monastic expression and leadership. The medieval period began after the split between the Catholic and Orthodox Churches in 1054 and this lasted until the Reformation in 1517, which released the evangelical church era including the birth of the Baptist, Methodist and Salvation Army movements and worldwide missionary activity. Which then brings us to the current age, which began in the Azusa Street Revival in 1906 and birthed the Pentecostal Church and a fresh under-standing of the work of the Holy Spirit which is growing rapidly across the world.

We can argue with Mumford's analysis, but the insight that I want to draw from his assessment is that these tectonic shifts take decades, even centuries, to be worked out. And I believe we have begun to see the signs of the significant shift into the new forms of church that God is birthing.

An equation

There is always a risk in trying to simplify things that are complex, and when it comes to God's kingdom, he refuses to be boxed in. But there is equally a danger that we are so overwhelmed by the change that is happening, we cannot understand it and are paralysed. Jesus seemed to give us permission to work from simple principles to understand complex situations when he said:

> 'When evening comes, you say, "It will be fair weather, for the sky is red," and in the morning, "Today it will be stormy, for the sky is red and overcast." You know how to interpret the appearance of the sky, but you cannot interpret the signs of the times.' (Matt. 16.2–3)

Just as the repeating pattern of a red sky preceding a storm helps people to understand the complexity of the weather systems, so there are 'signs' that we can interpret to understand the spiritual significance of what we are experiencing. So, what might those red sky signs of the kingdom be for us today? I am definitely not a mathematician, but I have always enjoyed the way that mathematical equations allow us to understand the complex combination of multiple factors that produce a particular outcome. So let me offer you an equation.

External crisis + inner conviction + God-given
momentum = church reformation

These are the common factors that have accompanied times of reformation.

External crisis

In 1988 the Choluteca Bridge was built in Honduras as an indestructible bridge to ensure the Choluteca River could always be crossed. Six months later Hurricane Mitch blew through the country with devastating effect. The bridge stood firm, but the landscape was unrecognizable, and the course of the river had moved, meaning the bridge no longer spanned the river and no longer fulfilled its purpose! The calling of the Church is to be a bridge between a God who created this world and loves it and people who are lost and unaware of his love and presence. The winds of societal change have blown through our nation and where the Church used to do that work of connecting people to God, in many situations it has been left disconnected and failing to fulfil its missionary purpose.

The denomination within which I am privileged to serve is the Church of England, which has experienced 70 years of continuous decline; in the last 20 years we have lost 48 per cent of our active members under the age of 18, and 24 per cent of all adults. The average age of someone worshipping in a Church of England church is 61, compared with the national average of 41. As Linda Woodhead wrote in the *Church Times*:

The Church's greatest failure in our lifetime has been its refusal to take decline seriously. The situation is now so grave that it is no longer enough simply to focus on making parts grow again. The whole structure needs to be reviewed from top to toe, and creative and courageous decisions need to be made.[4]

We have been moving into this crisis slowly over decades, but the recent Covid pandemic has accelerated it. The periods of lockdown and being locked out of our church buildings have revealed a poverty of discipleship on a macro scale, in which many people have realized their faith was essentially a Sunday service observance and involvement in church programmes. And the economic crisis that has accompanied the need for lockdowns has exposed several denominations to the financial crisis that they have been overlooking. It is no longer possible for historic resources to paper over the cracks and pay the costs of clergy and buildings that smaller congregations can no longer afford.

The society we are part of is also experiencing crisis. We are in a crisis of relationships and identity. At a national level, arguments over Brexit and Scottish Independence have split communities and nations. Internationally, issues of racial justice with the Black Lives Matter movement have caused us to look inside at the injustice that still exists in our communities. The Russian invasion of Ukraine has brought the human capacity for destruction and terror close to home. The climate change crisis demands change and yet rampant consumerism demands more consumption and is at the heart of the environmental threat to the future of the planet. And the inequalities of wealth between the poor and the rich are growing larger. The so-called sexual revolution has resulted in boundaryless expressions of sexuality, sexual relationships and identity. And we, in society and in the Church, have failed to keep the young and vulnerable safe from abuse. The promise of all these social freedoms was self-fulfilment and yet one of the most serious aspects of the crisis we face is the level of anxiety and mental health problems people are experiencing.

Jesus described this pain and the reality of being separated from God as being 'lost'. And his response was to say that he had not come to condemn the world but to seek and to save us. When you came to faith in Jesus, he left you in this world and commissioned you as part of his mission team, the Church. To pray and live the kingdom of heaven into every aspect of the world around you. You are the Church. We can't *go* to church; we can only *be* the Church. This is our purpose and calling, and this is why God is reforming us because we need to be fit for this purpose in a lost world that desperately needs him.

The following was written by W. T. Stead, an eyewitness of the 1904 Welsh Revival in which 100,000 people were saved within a year:

> It is ever the darkest hour before the dawn. The nation always seems to be given over to the Evil One before the coming of the Son of Man. The decay of religious faith, the deadness of the churches, the atheism of the well-to-do, the brutality of the masses, all these, when at their worst, herald the approach of the revival. Things seem to get too bad to last. The reign of evil becomes intolerable. Then the soul of the nation awakes.[5]

Inner conviction

In every time of reformation God has raised up people with a shared conviction that he was calling them to something different, to join in with a new work of his grace in that time and place. As the seriousness of our situation today begins to dawn, we also hear voices expressing hope that Jesus is reigning in glory and his commission to his Church to make disciples of all nations still stands. Anne Calver, who leads the Unleashed network of churches, recently shared her conviction that:

> God is getting his church ready for the harvest. And that there are two signs of this. A waking up of the church to what the Holy Spirit is doing and a reaching out to the lost and a longing for people to come to faith.[6]

I wonder if you relate to that?

As I listen to leaders across many different denominations I sense that there is a growing hunger for renewal. This is birthing a willingness and openness to doing something different. And there are thousands of people expressing this conviction in forming all kinds of new churches in every different context around the country. Every conversation like this and every new church are seeds of hope growing in people's hearts that are declaring, 'God hasn't finished with us yet.' When William Booth's daughter Catherine was pioneering the mission of the Salvation Army in France and facing great opposition, she wrote to him listing all the challenges. William reportedly replied by telegram and wrote, 'Take your eyes off the waves and see the rising tide.' So, despite the challenges we face, there is a growing tide of hope that God is going to renew his Church and empower us to fulfil our calling.

God-given momentum

It is into the place of desperation which crisis and conviction create that the Holy Spirit flows. The current conditions that I have described are exactly the kind of conditions in which God has poured out his revival fire in the past. This reformation is not a work of human ingenuity and effort. It is a work of the Holy Spirit. Without God moving we are in a situation of irreversible decline, but we are also ripe for revival. We will talk about revival later in this book, but this is the word people have used to describe that moment when God breaks in to do this reforming work. Often, we hold a 'rummage sale' to create more space. I think this reformation is about clearing away a lot of stuff that has built up that gets in the way of God, so that we can have more space for him. And that clearing of space is personal, within our hearts and lives, and within the cultures and practices of the Church. When that space and freedom open up, the momentum begins to build as God pours his Spirit into his Church. He has done it before and there is a growing hunger and expectation that he is going to do it again. So, while our society can now be labelled a post-Christian society, I prefer to describe it as a pre-revival society.

Reformation

'Reformation' has become a specialized historical term to describe the development of the Protestant churches and confession of faith in the sixteenth century. The term communicates the desire of Luther to see the existing Church transformed by his thesis and convictions. It was Karl Barth who popularized the Latin slogan *Ecclesia reformata, semper reformanda, est secundum verbum Dei*, 'The church reformed ought always to be reforming, according to the word of God.'[7] This reformed Protestant conviction that the Church never reaches its perfect form and must always be open to the ongoing work of reform by the Holy Spirit in accordance with his word. Reformation does not come from a rejection of the Church but a love for it and a desire to see us become all God intended us to be.

But, just as Luther experienced, every move of God has been resisted by people within the Church. John Wesley was an Anglican until his death and never intended to form a new denomination, but Methodism was born because the Anglican leadership at the time did not create space for the reviving work God was doing to grow and develop within its structures. And this makes the significance of what we are considering now even more important. Will we create the space God is asking us to and partner with him in his reforming work, or will we inadvertently resist him and discover we are in opposition to his work?

All things new

What the Church has often failed to realize is that renewing things is at the heart of who God is. The culmination of his saving work is not to discard this creation and start again, but to declare, 'I am making everything new' (Rev. 21.5). The Greek word for new used in this verse is *Kainos*. *Kainos* can mean a new form of something or something that is vastly improved from its previous state. *Kainos* is not rejecting the old and making something different; it is a transformed version of the old, something completely fresh. It expresses the quality of newness that something has.[8] It is just like the work that mechanics do in programmes like *Pimp My Ride*, where owners take their worn-out cars to the custom body shops and they are stripped back, transformed with new paintwork and every new gadget you can imagine. What emerges is still a car but it is unrecognizable when compared with the old. This is who God is; everything he touches he renews, and the big plan he has for his creation is to renew everything.

Remember the image we opened this book with? Well, it was given to a man called Simon Braker, one of the leadership team of the British Isles Council of Prophets. He is a close friend whom I trust and someone with a proven track record in prophetic ministry. He was given this word at the beginning of 2000 but at the beginning of 2020, before the Covid pandemic was known, he sensed that it was for this time and that the nation would go through a time of desolation, from which the future Church will emerge.

God often speaks through prophets by giving a vivid image that gets his people's attention. But then we have to discern the practical outworking of this in our lives. The idea of church structures being smashed is a challenge to us to take what God is doing seriously, and the first thing we have to realize is that this is part of the work God does. We see it in Jesus overturning the tables in the temple; the traders serving the sacrificial system had moved into the space provided for the Gentiles to be included in the temple and Jesus refused to allow anything to remain that would get in the way of people connecting with God (Matt. 21.12–17). Jesus is so strong and violent as he makes a whip and drives the traders from the temple courts because he knows they will not give up their established places and patterns willingly. C. S. Lewis describes it in this way:

> My idea of God is not a divine idea. It has to be shattered from time to time. He shatters it Himself. He is the great iconoclast. Could we not almost say that this shattering is one of the marks of His presence?[9]

At times Jesus becomes the great disruptor of his people. And at these times God asks us to surrender everything to him and bring our lives and the patterns and practices of our Church to him, allowing him to reform anything that no longer serves him and his kingdom.

Change your mind!

So, there is hope in the ruins that Jesus is at the centre of all we are going through and inviting us to join him in the dance. And those factors of external crisis, inner conviction and God-given momentum are creating a rhythm that many are beginning to feel and our feet are starting to move. So how do we respond to what God is doing?

Jesus arrived in the midst of God's people who were oppressed and compromised by the Roman rule of Jerusalem, failing to care for the poor and marginalized, and fighting among themselves. Nothing spiritual of any note had happened for over 400 years (there it is again!), and his message was, 'Repent for the kingdom of God is near.' *Metanoia* is the Greek word used to describe Jesus' call for repentance, and this is the way Jesus issues his invitation to follow him, because it is first of all a step of change. It's a call to turn away from our sins, but the meaning of the word is deeper than just sorrow for sin; it reveals that this happens when we see things differently in the light of Jesus. *Metanoia* is about stopping, examining the direction we are heading in, recognizing the need for change, and turning around to face a new direction.[10] And new directions are full of potential, loaded with new possibilities. And new possibilities bring new futures.

If the advances of science had made it possible, I would now reach into your brain and erase any memory you connect with the word 'church', so that when you hear that word there is no default setting defining what you think of when you hear it. The reason for this is because, as the ancient philosopher Epictetus explained, 'it is impossible for a person to learn what they think they already know'.[11] Jesus is inviting us to reimagine what it means to be the Church. But our minds can become fixed in a particular way of thinking and this framework will not allow any hope that things could be different to penetrate it. This way of thinking prevents us from engaging with the renewing work of God in his Church.

This is what Ed Silvoso describes as a stronghold. He says that: 'A spiritual stronghold is a mindset impregnated with hopelessness that causes us to accept as unchangeable, situations that we know are contrary to the will of God.'[12] It is important to understand that we do not have to change and turn around in every area of our Christian life. But where our thought patterns and practices become rigid in ways that will resist the new things God is doing, Jesus is calling us to repent.

A vision of the future

I genuinely believe the best days of the Church in the United Kingdom are ahead of us. But they won't look like the best days by the current standards or measurement of success that we use today: size and numbers and our position and influence in society. I believe they will be characterized by the Church being marginalized, organizationally weakened and humbled and on our knees before God; these are the places God has always begun his work of revival. The following chapters will not describe what I think the future Church should look like but will give you some landmarks to navigate this new territory by, the landmarks that we find consistently in four contexts in which the Church has gone through similar times of change.

First, Scripture, where we find the pattern of the Church that Jesus established as he called his disciples to follow him and birthed through the pouring out of his Spirit. The history of Christian movements and revivals reveals that many of them are a result of a rediscovery of early Christian belief and practice. The book of Acts is not just a historical record; it is a manual for revival. As the great revivalist Aimee Semple McPherson said: 'Awake! thou that sleepest, arise from the dead! The Lord still lives today. His power has never abated. His Word has never changed. The things He did in Bible days, He still lives to do today.'[13] The book of Ephesians gives us a big picture of God's glory revealed in Jesus Christ and his relationship with his Church, and so we will engage with this letter as a thread running through *The Church of Tomorrow*.

Second, Church history. How has God historically brought revival and transformed his Church and society? We must study these examples, not to copy their forms and patterns but to learn the ways of God. One of the weaknesses of today's Church is a historical amnesia. This work of interpreting history and translating it into today's context will be at the heart of our discernment about the future. It is fascinating that where the Church is alive and growing it seems either to be renewing ancient practices of contemplation or stepping into Pentecostal Holy Spirit power; both of these are a renewal of something the Church has lost. As Leonard Sweet helps us to understand in his book *Post-Modern Pilgrims*, we will need to hold the past and the present in conversation so that the Church in the future is an expression of the gospel that has been entrusted to us.[14]

Third, outside of Western countries, around the world the Church is growing rapidly. This tells us that the gospel still works, God's Spirit has not been withdrawn and growth is experienced when the Church is set free from restrictions. It is estimated that every day more than 100,000 people globally come to faith in Christ and hundreds of churches are planted. In 1910 about two-thirds of the world's Christians lived in Europe. Today, more than 1.3 billion Christians now live in the Global South (61 per cent) compared with 860 million in the Global North (39 per cent).[15] We need the humility to learn from our sisters and brothers from the vibrant Church elsewhere in the world.

Finally, the prophets. God does nothing without first telling his servants the prophets (Amos 3.7). I appreciate that the role of the prophet is not universally understood or accepted in the Church today, but the work of God's Spirit within his people across the world is producing a consistent 'sound' that God is calling his Church at this time to get ready for reformation.

Below are the landmarks that I believe will mark the Church in the future, and each one is explored in a chapter of this book. Though sometimes already present, the reformation God is beginning will mean that these practices will become the marks of the Church of tomorrow and the core business of every follower of Christ. And they are not independent of one another. Each practice opens the door for us to deepen our understanding of the next.

The Church of tomorrow . . .

- honours Jesus as Lord
- is dependent upon the Holy Spirit
- is confident in the gospel
- is a disciple-making community
- plants churches that will plant churches
- has a diverse leadership

- is a holy people
- prioritizes prayer.

My prayer is that not only will you engage with the big shifts God is bringing to his Church, but you will also experience the personal renewal Jesus is always wanting to bring to our lives. We need a personal conviction that God hasn't finished with his Church, to strengthen us for the journey of reformation, which is why each chapter concludes with a guided personal response that will aid you as you think and pray. As we read and consider, we will need humility and hope. Humility to allow God to do whatever he needs to do with us and hope to keep us moving forward. When Desmond Tutu was asked if he was an optimist he replied, 'I'm not optimistic, no I'm quite different. I'm hopeful, I am a prisoner of hope.'[16]

An invitation

In the Lord's compassion and gentleness, he prefers to issue invitations rather than dictates, and as we begin our journey, I want to include a beautiful invitation to join the dance and say yes to being part of the work of reformation of his Church. It comes from the book of Song of Songs, and it picks up the images of trellis and prison bars that we have used. And through the latticework of a window the Lord appears and speaks words of affirmation and love, and words of hope that the winter is over, and it is now a change of season in which he calls his Church to arise and leave her restrictions and be free.

My beloved is like a gazelle or a young stag. Look! There he stands behind our wall, gazing through the windows, peering through the lattice. My beloved spoke and said to me, 'Arise, my darling, my beautiful one, come with me. See! The winter is past; the rains are over and gone. Flowers appear on the earth; the season of singing has come, the cooing of doves is heard in our land. The fig tree forms its early fruit; the blossoming vines spread their fragrance. Arise, come, my darling; my beautiful one, come with me.' (Song of Songs 2.9–13)

Personal response: repentance and trust

Read: Ephesians 1.1–2.

Paul, an apostle of Christ Jesus by the will of God,
To God's holy people in Ephesus, the faithful in Christ Jesus:
Grace and peace to you from God our Father and the Lord
    Jesus Christ.

Take a few moments of silence and some deep breaths. Spend a few moments of prayer in thanks for the gifts of God's grace and peace in your life.

As Paul begins this letter he writes 'To God's holy people in Ephesus, the faithful in Christ Jesus'. In talking about the Church, he emphasizes two qualities, 'holy' and 'faithful'. 'Holy' means that the people are set apart, blessed with a calling and a purpose that is God centred. They are 'faithful' because they are seeking to obey and follow Jesus. And to his Church Paul explains God has gifts of grace and peace.

In response to Paul's description of the Ephesians as 'holy' and 'faithful', ask God whether this could be a true description of you and the church you are part of. Bring your thoughts honestly to God in this time and repent of anything that you realize needs to change. And then ask for his grace to follow him and receive his peace.

Finish by reading this prayer of Thomas Merton, making it your own:

My Lord God, I have no idea where I am going. I do not see the road ahead of me. I cannot know for certain where it will end. Nor do I really know myself and the fact that I think that I am following your will does not mean that I am actually doing so. But I believe that the desire to please you does in fact please you. And I hope I have that desire in all that I am doing. I hope that I will never do anything apart from that desire. And I know that if I do this you will lead me by the right road though I may know nothing about it. Therefore, will I trust you always though I may seem to be lost and in the shadow of death. I will not fear, for you are ever with me, and you will never leave me to face my perils alone. Amen.[17]

1

Jesus is Lord

How can you live with the terrifying thought that the hurricane has become human, that the fire has become flesh, that life itself came to life and walked in our midst? Christianity either means that, or it means nothing. It is either the more devastating disclosure of the deepest reality in the world, or it's a sham, a nonsense, a bit of deceitful play-acting. Most of us, unable to cope with saying either of those things, condemn ourselves to live in the shallow world in between.

—N. T. Wright[1]

Jesus is Lord! BOOM. Drop the mic. There's nothing left to say. The whole of the Christian faith is contained in these three words. Nothing of our faith makes sense without them and everything we believe flows from them. Paul used it as the declaration that everyone must make to receive Christ's salvation: 'If you declare with your mouth, "Jesus is Lord," and believe in your heart that God raised him from the dead, you will be saved' (Rom. 10.9). It was the response of worship by his friends to the resurrected Jesus, 'My Lord and my God' (John 20.28). It was the cry of the early Christians that turned the whole of their world upside down. It is the confession of the persecuted Church today. And this is the standard that God is calling us to live and die by again.

As Frost and Hirsch write:

The church's elemental confession that 'Jesus is Lord' captures all the meaning and significance of the biblical teaching on the kingdom of God . . . Our view of God is that Jesus is Lord, and the kingdom of God is the arena in which we respond to God's sovereign rule over this world. All is included (and nothing is excluded) in this claim.[2]

The danger is that as we read these three words, we read them as a theological statement. They are actually a cry of joy and worship from a community passionate about Jesus, captivated by his majesty and the life and love he has poured into their lives. Or they can be more of a war cry or act of defiance. To declare them over our lives is much more like *Alba gu bràth!* or 'Scotland Forever!', as used by Scottish sports fans or freedom fighters. We are declaring that nothing else, no idol or ambition, will ever dethrone Jesus from his glorious rule over creation and from being Lord of our lives. And we are surrendering to his rule and committing to serve his purposes in this world. The lordship of Jesus Christ extends over our finances, our family, our work, our play, our ambitions, our politics, our sexuality and everything in between.

When the lordship of Jesus is settled as a question in a Christian's life all other issues are settled. It is stating that Jesus has a claim on every part of us, without limits. Jesus says, 'You are mine' over every part of our lives. But the opposite is also true, as Zwemer first said, 'Unless Jesus is Lord of all, he is not Lord at all.'[3] We cannot overstate how important this is: everything stands or falls upon our response to Jesus' call for us to make him Lord of our lives.

Come and follow me

If Jesus began his public ministry with a call for repentance, he began the work of forming the new kingdom community, the Church, with the simple call, 'Come, follow me . . . and I will send you out to fish for people' (Mark 1.17). Those simple words to four young fishermen were a loving and gracious invitation into relationship with him. But the nature of that relationship was established right from the beginning: Jesus was in charge. To follow him involved submitting every area of their lives to him and allowing him to set the purpose and agenda of every day. They left everything and followed him. Up until that moment the height of their ambition was to be married, take on their fathers' business and catch as many fish as they could every day. They were not the spiritual elite of the synagogue youth group who would have been spotted by other Jewish rabbis. These were the ordinary Jewish boys who hadn't made the grade. Jesus saw in them the potential to be world changers but the only way that would happen would be if they put him in charge of their lives. From that day onwards they were to learn from him.

Skip forward three years and the first witnesses of the resurrected Jesus ran from the garden and announced to the disciples, 'I have seen the Lord!' (John 20.18, 25). Those three years were a journey of realization that Jesus was not just their Lord, but THE Lord. And following those first disciples, 'Jesus is Lord' was the cry of the early Church. We know this because a personal privatized religion that had no external effect on a person's behaviour or allegiances would have been no threat at all to the surrounding Roman culture. But 'Jesus is Lord' directly confronted the popular Roman declaration 'Caesar is Lord'. The early Christians believed that if Jesus of Nazareth was risen and ascended to glory then no one else could be lord over him, and therefore no one could overrule his authority and he was to be obeyed.

The apostle Paul was executed in Rome years later under the regime of Nero. Paul wasn't imprisoned and executed for defending the theory or philosophy of the Christian faith, but for declaring an allegiance that had a higher authority in his life than Rome. This conviction turned the world upside down, as the city of Ephesus experienced when Paul's proclamation of Jesus as Lord dethroned Artemis (Acts 19.23–41). The early Church's belief in Jesus as Lord was a subversive counter narrative to the world around them and it challenged any belief or practice that did not submit to Christ. To be the Church of tomorrow that Jesus is calling us to be we need to return and rebuild this foundation. We are to be the community surrendered to Jesus and filled with him so that we can be used by him to bring about his kingdom on the earth.

Ephesians teaches the supremacy of Christ as all things will be fulfilled in him (1.10), that he is the head over all things (1.22–23) and his glory is the goal of the Church (3.21). The reformation that the Church experiences at different times is always a returning to being Jesus' people. It is first of all a re-founding of our lives upon Jesus before it becomes a reforming. The question for us is whether we are allowing the truth of Jesus' lordship to transform our lives. Are we living under that story of his life and loving sacrifice, his resurrection and ascension and his rule over all things? Because that is the story we are called to live out in our everyday lives.

The alternative is what A. W. Tozer termed 'Christless Christianity'[4] in which Jesus is celebrated as Saviour but rejected as Lord. This is where we 'consume' the benefits of all that Jesus is on our terms and do not offer him the throne of our lives. We reduce Jesus to a form that we can manage, or which reflects the kind of Lord we are looking for. A reduced and limited Jesus doesn't require everything from us and is much more manageable than the Lord of the universe. The problem is that it just isn't Jesus. And Jesus refuses to be contained. He demands that we accept his divine and sovereign claim upon our lives as Lord.

The Christendom cataract

'What can you see?' I asked Maria. 'Everything!' she replied. 'I can read every word.' And she proceeded to read every word of a Bible verse in Portuguese written on the sanctuary wall of the church 20 metres away. We were now both crying. Maria had come to ask me to pray for her because she was completely blind from cataracts that had grown across her eyes. We were in a church in São Paulo in Brazil, and I was part of the team offering to pray for people. Maria had come explaining that she wanted Jesus to heal her from the cataracts that had blinded her. She could not afford medical treatment to have them removed. And so I prayed and declared healing in Jesus' name. We prayed twice with no signs of any results. But Maria encouraged me to keep seeking God. And then on the third time she began to see some light. And now after the fifth time of intense prayer she could see clearly. The cataracts had disappeared. Jesus had healed her. Praise his name.

I share this story first to give testimony that Jesus is Lord of all. In his reign over all things, he is Lord over all sickness and as he brings his kingly reign into a situation, he transforms it. But I also share it as a metaphor for what I believe needs to happen in the Church. In his book *Mere Discipleship* Lee Camp talks about the 'cataract of Christendom'[5] that still affects the Church. What Camp means by this is that beliefs and practices which grew up during the time of Christendom have distorted the Christian faith and 'blind' the Church today. Like Maria we can get on with our lives and practise our Christian faith, but unlike Maria we are unaware of the blindness that affects us. Just as a cataract gradually grows across a person's eye and eventually robs them of sight, so the pattern of the Christian faith that we accept as normal and normative has developed over centuries and we are now unaware that there could be an alternative. We need to recover our vision of the Church as Jesus established it.

The word 'Christendom' came to be used to describe the place where the Christian religion was the dominant world view and culture. It is an Anglo-Saxon term which appears to have first been used in the ninth century by a scribe at the court of King Alfred the Great of Wessex, who found he needed a way to describe the idea of the universal culture focused on Jesus Christ. That was the state of English culture from that time until the Enlightenment began to undermine universal acceptance of the Christian faith in the eighteenth century. The general acceptance of the goodness of the Christian faith brought great blessings to our society as people lived generally in accordance with God's will. But at the same time the practice of the Christian faith became distorted in a number of significant ways.

The distortions that developed came from two fundamental flaws. First, people assumed that the values of the world lined up with the values of the kingdom of God. The Christian faith built up such a strong influence over the society's structures, laws and cultural norms that we developed a relationship of collaboration and partnership with the world. And because of this pattern of relationship, as the values of the world began to change, subtly but significantly, the world began to set the Church's practice and agenda. And this is a significant threat to the Church now that the values of our post-Christian society have diverged significantly from the Christian faith.

The second flaw was that the Church stopped being a missionary enterprise within our society because we assumed everyone was 'Christian'. Even though there were times of significant decline in attendance at Sunday services and moral decline, the Church still baptized, married and buried most people and there was no general sense of the responsibility to evangelize within the Church. The mission of bringing in Jesus' rule and reign in people's lives became the work of specialists, whose job it was to export the Christian faith to the worlds where the British Empire was expanding to 'convert the heathen'. Evangelism and mission to our own culture and people slipped from the core business of the Church. And so, the predominant culture and practice of the Christian faith did not include a missionary call for believers to be missional disciples who make new followers of Jesus. And we are now reaping the results of this flaw. We live in a society that generally sees the Church and

Jesus as irrelevant to people's lives and so our modus operandi must be that we are constantly 'on mission', but the Church has little experience of living like this.

No longer a collaborating majority?

At this time in our history, I believe Jesus is giving us an invitation to imagine a different way of being the Church. But it involves a choice. And the option Jesus is giving us is to follow him along an unfamiliar path where the direction and destination are unknown. All that we will know is that our Lord is leading us and will be forming and shaping us as we follow him. The alternative is that we seek to stay on well-known paths. It is a very tempting route as it minimizes change and has the comforts of familiar patterns and the apparent security of us feeling competent because we know how to do church in this way. We need the past and we must steward its wisdom and treasures, but we must not let ourselves become imprisoned by it or let it become an idol. The danger is that, like the Israelites who at the first struggle of their new-found freedom began to long for the familiarity of slavery in Egypt, we will feel nostalgic about Christendom's patterns and privileges. But Christendom is over, and Jesus wants his Church back.

The Christendom church can be characterized as a *collaborating majority*, where we occupied a privileged position within society and the values of the Christian faith were held by most of the people. In mid-twentieth-century Britain we began to see that we had shifted to the *conflicted middle* that we occupy today. This has happened because of the winds of societal change where organized religion is now distrusted, individual freedom is celebrated, and the use of that freedom has led people to beliefs and practices that are contrary to the Christian faith. Our society rejects as oppressive any system that requires specific beliefs and practices that curtail individual freedom and challenge a person's right to independently define their identity. Yet that is who Jesus is; he is our Lord, and he lovingly calls us to obey him and find our identity in him. The cultural frame of reference has shifted so dramatically that it now accepts what Root calls 'the immanent frame' which 'leads us to see things as mostly, if not completely, natural and material'.[6] And in this frame of reference there is little room for the transcendent or divine.

So, we now feel the tension of being caught in the middle, between being the Church the world wants us to be and the Jesus-shaped community we are called to be. There is still significant engagement with the Church in some of the fantastic ways that we serve our communities in toddler groups, food banks, schools work, lunch clubs for the elderly and so on. Yet there is now little knowledge of who Jesus is and what it means to follow him. And we struggle to know how to communicate the goodness of Jesus to others when his ways are so different from those of the world. This transitional and conflicted space feels deeply uncomfortable as we are confronted with multiple and confusing choices about the Church, our identity and calling.

A compromised mythology?

There is a fork in the road approaching for each of us as Christians and the Church as a whole. The choices before us are complex and nuanced, but can be bluntly described as two paths leading to two very different destinations.

The first path leads to a possible destination of the Church being a *compromised mythology*. We can continue to sleepwalk into the future hoping that our society still wants us to be its social conscience and civic service providers. But, in order to fulfil that role, we will increasingly have to remove anything that challenges the values of the world. In our desire to care for people and have influence we will have to be silent about Jesus' call to repent and believe in him. We will personalize our faith so that it is reduced to a privatized religion that we are not expected to live out explicitly or share with others. And within the Church Jesus will no longer be able to be the glorious Lord of all creation reigning in authority over us, but instead he will have to become a mythic figure whose life and teachings are an illustration to guide us. He will be the patron saint of the Church, a figurehead who represents the God to whom we pray, but alongside other examples and gurus. He will remain precious to us, but we will have stripped him of his life-transforming power. The revelation held within the Bible, Jesus' word to us, will no longer be held as the highest form of revelation, but instead progressive human revelation will be the authority in this Church. The loving service so many churches offer to our communities will go on, but with little distinctive Christian witness or emphasis on leading people to know Jesus Christ. Willian Inge wrote, shortly after becoming Dean of St Paul's Cathedral in 1911, 'If you marry the spirit of your own generation you will be a widow in the next.'[7] This is because if we allow culture to shape our values and beliefs the Church will lose touch with the fullness of Jesus. And then we will discover the culture in the future continues to move on again and rejects the Church and we are left in no-man's-land. The fundamental problem is that in this scenario Jesus is no longer Lord of his Church. And all we will have to offer the world is ourselves.

Without Jesus as Lord our worship becomes vulnerable to being idolatrous, in which we focus on the physical order of things and performance of worship and put ourselves and our experience of worship at the centre instead of Jesus. We become the centre of the story. The lordship of Jesus becomes eclipsed by collusion with the world and loyalty to the tradition of the Church. And let me be clear, I have seen this in both cathedrals and charismatic warehouses and so it is not an issue of one particular tradition. As Kierkegaard put it:

The established church is far more dangerous to Christianity than any heresy or schism. We play at Christianity. We use all the orthodox Christian terminology – but everything, everything without character. Yes, we are simply not fit to shape a heresy or a schism. There is something frightful in the fact that the most dangerous thing of all, playing at Christianity, is never included in the list of heresies or schisms.[8]

Or a creative minority?

The alternative destination is one that Jon Tyson and Heather Grizzle call a *creative minority*.[9] Here we live out the lordship of Jesus in a creative and engaging way. We dare to claim that the biblical narrative is THE story we are all called to live under and that it is the only story offering the ultimate meaning, purpose and direction of human history in Jesus Christ. And we offer this wonderful story to those around us in fresh and creative ways, but without compromise. We refuse to separate ourselves from the world around us and to become a narrow sect because we know that Jesus loves the world, and he is the Lord who renews all things. We are, as Jesus prayed we would be, not of the world but still in it (John 17.15–17). We give up worrying about our status and reputation, and instead we are a non-anxious community, and happy to be on the margins rather than at the centre of society, living alongside people and seeking to love our neighbours. We acknowledge we have nothing of ourselves to offer the world and instead we simply share Jesus with them in word and deed because he is the one who gives life and renews us. We seek to break through the distortions of the immanent frame and present a picture of life and the world with Jesus transcendent in his glory and reigning personally over our lives.

Within our changing world this will be incredibly attractive to some and deeply offensive to others. Jesus warned us that the world will hate us just as it hated him (John 15.18). The cost of this is that the Church can no longer be the unifying centre of our culture. Instead, alongside loving and serving others, we will cause offence, be a distinctive prophetic voice and operate from the margins and not the centre. We will be smaller and humbler. This is what it means to be a minority. Sounds a bit like Jesus, doesn't it? The carpenter from Nazareth who held no position of power or political office, had no formal educational qualification and never travelled more than 200 miles from his birthplace. But, also like Jesus, we have to learn how to bring the love, truth and power of God creatively to connect with the lives of those around us. To challenge oppressive and restrictive systems. To offer his re-creating power into every situation of brokenness in people's lives around us. And then to see how this spreads from one person to another and transforms them and their relationships. And the way that happens is in communities who make Jesus Lord and allow his re-creating presence to shape them so that they embody good news to those around them and invite others to join them.

Chief Rabbi Jonathan Sacks wrote:

To become a creative minority is not easy because it involves maintaining strong links with the outside world while staying true to your faith, seeking not merely to keep the sacred flame burning but also to transform the larger society of which you are a part. This is a demanding and risk laden choice.[10]

We have to return to the early Church for what this looks like. Here we find a Church that is living out its faith radically. People who are abiding in Christ and living in the fullness of life that Jesus offers, praying passionately, loving sacrificially, ministering supernaturally and believing for the impossible. It is a life lived in the deep end. It is costly and it only makes sense if Jesus is Lord. It refuses to compromise in order to achieve popularity and position. And this is why Paul wrote from prison to urge those early Christians 'to live a life worthy of the calling you have received' (Eph. 4.1), a calling to follow Jesus.

Creative communities

The Church as a whole will be this creative minority within the wider society. But the way this will manifest is in many cells of the body of Christ all over the nation coming alive in Jesus, living out the kingdom under his lordship in their contexts and communities. These creative communities will be wonderfully diverse as they express new forms of worship, prayer and life of the Church; they will listen to the voice of Jesus and the people around them and incarnate the good news of Jesus in their neighbourhoods.

The concept of a creative minority connects with what the Bible talks about as a remnant. Throughout the history of God's work with his people he has chosen to form a remnant, a smaller community of people who remain faithful to God despite the culture around them, and through them he brings about revival. It is Noah and his family, and Daniel and his friends, the exiles who returned with Ezra and Nehemiah, Jesus and his disciples, and the 120 gathered in the upper room on the day of Pentecost. Or in more recent history where a few people began to pray for revival, such as the Moravians in Germany, the Wesleys or Evan Roberts and his friends before the Welsh Revival. And so these small cells where Jesus is Lord and his Spirit is releasing creativity and faith will be within wider church communities that are still in the contested middle, calling more and more people to join the dance.

In the early sixth century a young man called Benedict travelled from a small central Italian town called Nursia to Rome. Half a century earlier Rome had been sacked by the barbarians and Rome had fallen from its greatness. Benedict was shocked by the vice and corruption of Rome. So, he retreated as a young man to the Simbruinian hills and later to a cave in the rocks beside the lake then existing near the ruins of Nero's palace above Subiaco, 40 miles east of Rome. There he lived alone for three years, with food and simple monastic clothes provided by Romanus, a monk of one of the monasteries nearby. By the time Benedict emerged from the cave his reputation for holiness and nearness to God had spread and he was invited to be abbot of a nearby monastic community. To guide the monks Benedict wrote a simple book of guidance which came to be known as the Rule of St Benedict, what Benedict described as 'a school for the Lord's service'.[11] It had three distinct vows: obedience, stability (commitment to the same monastic community until death) and conversion of life (the lifelong work of repentance). The renewal of devotion and faith that Benedict brought led to the growth of monasteries in that region as many people left their lives in the world and devoted themselves to serving Christ. These communities became centres of restoration and learning. They evangelized the barbarians, taught them how to pray and plant crops and to build. All from the seed of faith and devotion God had planted in Benedict. He had no intention of starting a movement; he simply wanted to devote himself to God.

It serves as an example of what a small community of believers who respond with faith and devotion and creativity can be used by God to do. Rod Dreher in his book *The Benedict Option* argues that the present cultural moment in which we find ourselves in the West resonates with the time of the fall of the Roman Empire.[12] The chaos of the Dark Ages that followed the barbarian invasion is the equivalent to the culture of self-interest and moral relativism of our day. And Dreher contends that we can learn from Benedict, who constructed new forms of community within which faith and moral life could be sustained. In the midst of the disorientation and confusion we are experiencing, forming these communities can provide reservoirs of resilience as we nurture a culture of faith, hope and love. Alastair MacIntyre suggests that we need 'another – doubtless very different – St Benedict'.[13] We actually need thousands of Benedicts who will come and lead these creative church communities.

In my work for the Gregory Centre for Church Multiplication I have the privilege of seeing them emerge. We are seeking to serve the planting of thousands of these creative communities led by ordinary people who sense that call from God to see something new emerge. I think of Bernice forming Wave Church to offer a church community which would include adults with learning difficulties. Or my friend Andy who is blind and planted a church during the Covid lockdown by hosting Facebook prayer evenings for his local estate and now runs a food store, church and discipleship community. Or Fiona who was walking her dog on a new housing estate and felt God call her to pray for it. From a pop-up café and Alpha course came a church and community drop-in that is the centre of that community. These are the creative minorities that God is raising up across the country.

Fix your eyes upon Jesus

Professor Robert Dale wrote a seminal work on renewing organizations, entitled *To Dream Again*. His revealing observation is that institutions generally follow a 'life cycle'. And when they begin to experience decline, they have a choice about how to respond. The typical response is to adopt restructuring solutions, adapting our current practice and nostalgically defending our position. Sadly, evidence suggests that these merely accelerate decline! In sharp contrast, Dale identifies healthy responses at this point that require reverting right back to the original concept that released the initial energy and creativity . . . 'the Founding Dream'.[14] The founding vision and commission of Jesus was to follow him. And whenever, in the past 2,000 years, we've returned to this founding dream, restorative movements have emerged.

There are no well-worn paths into the future. And the complexity can be overwhelming. But that is the joy of knowing Jesus as Lord. It is in surrender at his feet that we find a place of peace and hope. It is liberating to be able to give up relying on ourselves and instead completely trust Jesus and allow him to lead us into the future. 'And let us run with perseverance the race marked out for us, fixing our eyes on Jesus, the pioneer and perfecter of faith' (Heb. 12.1–2).

Personal response: surrender

Read: Ephesians 1.19–23.

> That power is the same as the mighty strength he exerted when he raised Christ from the dead and seated him at his right hand in the heavenly realms, far above all rule and authority, power and dominion, and every name that is invoked, not only in the present age but also in the one to come. And God placed all things under his feet and appointed him to be head over everything for the church, which is his body, the fullness of him who fills everything in every way.

Take some time to reflect on Jesus and who he is, his complete authority and power. Pray for the Lord to show you himself and make his presence known to you.

Thank God that Jesus has invited you to be a member of his body, the Church. Receive that invitation and commit yourself to follow him.

Ask him with whom you could begin to share what he is saying to you and with whom you could pray about what it might mean to be a creative minority in the midst of your community.

'Suscipe' (from the Latin word for 'receive') is a short but powerful prayer attributed to St Ignatius Loyola. It can be found towards the end of his *Spiritual Exercises*, first published in the sixteenth century.[15] St Ignatius helped found the Society of Jesus in the sixteenth century to serve the mission of the Church; this society is better known as the Jesuits.

Take, O Lord, and receive my entire liberty, my memory, my understanding and my whole will. All that I am and all that I possess, Thou hast given me: I surrender it all to Thee to be disposed of according to Thy will. Give me only Thy love and Thy grace; with these I will be rich enough and will desire nothing more. Amen.

2

Dependent upon the Holy Spirit

The Church was never intended to be a natural and intellectual organization, but a supernatural instrumentality wholly dependent upon the power of God.

—A. W. Tozer[1]

In 2020 Catherine Boone died prematurely aged 49, homeless and alone due to mental health difficulties and drug addiction. What followed her death was an inquest into why a woman who had struggled with these challenges had not accessed the $800,000 she had inherited from a relative who had died years before.

When Paul commanded the believers in Ephesus to 'be filled with the Spirit' (Eph. 5.18), he revealed a terrifying truth: it is possible to be a follower of Jesus Christ and not be living in the fullness of the Holy Spirit whom God has poured out upon his Church and who is available to every single Christian believer. Like Catherine Boone, sadly much of the Church today fails to realize the riches of the deposit of the Holy Spirit placed within her and within each Christian.

The early Church

Jesus' teaching recorded in John 13–17, often known as the upper room discourse, is seen by many as his greatest teaching. Why? Because, uniquely in the Gospel accounts, here Jesus was teaching about how his followers were to have a relationship with him and the Father through the person and presence of the Holy Spirit. He was preparing to ascend to heaven and he promised them the gift of the Spirit. Incredibly, Jesus said that this life would be better for them than if he remained physically with them (John 16.7), because his Spirit would come and dwell within them. And through the Spirit they would have Jesus and the Father dwelling in them, and through the Spirit they would do even greater things than Jesus (John 14.12–14). From this they knew that if they weren't going to have Jesus with them physically, they needed his Spirit living within them. And Jesus' words were not just for those first followers. He was describing our lives today. In John 13–17 Jesus is speaking into a future which is our present reality. And he is setting out the picture of what it means to follow him and make him Lord: it is a work of the Spirit. If we are to be a creative minority, Jesus says, we need the fullness of the Holy Spirit.

After Jesus' ascension the first disciples lived for ten days without the Spirit's presence and power filling them. They waited and prayed until the Spirit was poured out upon them on the day of Pentecost. Before that day they had wondered how they would manage to live out the commission Jesus had given them. After that day nothing could stop them. The contrast was night and day. And the Holy Spirit's presence and power was the mark of that first church. The early Church experienced him filling them (Acts 2), healing through them (Acts 3), shaking them (Acts 4), speaking to them (Acts 10.19; 13.1–3) and leading them (Acts 10; 11; 16.6–10). They had no formal and organized New Testament to read and to guide them. They were following the Spirit-inspired teaching of the apostles and the early Church fathers, and it was the leading of the Holy Spirit that they sought in every circumstance and his power and presence that allowed them to fulfil their mission. The result was that the communities they lived in were transformed: Jerusalem, Antioch, Ephesus. They were the example of being a minority within their context, bringing the kingdom of God in the power of the Spirit. Like them, as the Church of tomorrow, we desperately need to be marked by his presence among us and completely reliant on his love, revelation and power.

Biblical foundations

The eternal reign of Jesus in its fullness will renew all things. Jesus describes it in Matthew 19.28–29 when he says 'at the renewal of all things, when the Son of Man sits on his glorious throne'. To describe 'the renewal of all things' he uses a Greek word, *palingenesia*. This was a technical term describing the Greek belief that history was cyclical and every now and again there was a moment in which the world was purged, and history would start again. In other words, the world would be regenerated.[2] Jesus is explaining that the Greek philosophers were wrong. There is only one *palingenesia*, there is one final regeneration of the world, and it won't be just a reset of history; it will be the end of all death, and suffering, and sin and evil when he establishes his reign in glory, and in that moment he will renew all things.

Then, in Titus 3.5–6, Paul is writing about the new birth that the Holy Spirit works in a new believer. He writes, 'He saved us through the washing of rebirth [or: regeneration] and renewal by the Holy Spirit, whom he poured out on us generously through Jesus Christ our Saviour.' And remarkably, the term he uses to describe this 'regeneration' is the word *palingenesia*. So what Paul is saying is that the power God will use to renew the whole universe at the end of time is the same Holy Spirit who is renewing us. And so the potential for the Church to be the means by which God brings his kingdom on earth and renews and transforms communities is because we have the renewing *palingenesia* power of God within us. The reason we can trust that as we give up human position and influence there is hope for the future Church is because God has poured out his renewing presence in us and has withheld nothing from us.

This is a recurrent theme within the New Testament, that the fullness of the power of God has been made available to us. God knew that we would struggle to believe it and so he said it again and again. Paul writes about this three times to the Ephesians (1.22–23; 3.19; 4.15), and here he prays that they would know, 'That power is the same as the mighty strength he exerted when he raised Christ from the dead and seated him at his right hand in the heavenly realms' (Eph. 1.19–20).

The same power that raised Jesus from the dead is in us. Wow! But it raises a question: why do we as Christians and the Church seem so weak? And so we come back to Paul's commandment to the Ephesians to be filled with the Holy Spirit: 'Do not get drunk on wine, which leads to debauchery. Instead, be filled with the Spirit' (Eph. 5.18). Paul is giving his wake-up call to the Ephesian Christians and presenting them with a choice about how they live their lives. Will they be filled with the Spirit? There is nothing lacking on God's side of the equation; he has poured out his Spirit and withheld nothing. The question is whether they will choose to drink of him instead of the world. He compares being filled with the Spirit to being drunk on wine. One of the English phrases to describe someone who is drunk is 'being under the influence' as the alcohol begins to change their behaviour. And that is what God wants his Church to be: completely under his influence as the Holy Spirit's presence and power becomes the one shaping our lives and behaviour. So the question is not so much, 'Do you have the Holy Spirit?' but rather, 'How much of you does the Holy Spirit have?'

Personal experience

When Paul was in Ephesus he asked the Ephesian believers, 'Did you receive the Holy Spirit?' (Acts 19.2). This reveals something remarkable. That when we are filled with the Holy Spirit something happens; it is impossible to remain unchanged by the presence of

Almighty God filling our very beings. Yet I know so many good and faithful Christians who have no experience of the Spirit filling them, and they wonder why they are struggling to live the Christian life. You will probably be familiar with John Wesley's diary entry recording how the Spirit filled him and his 'heart was strangely warmed'.[3] But what is not often quoted is that he testifies to the result of this experience of transformation:

> And herein I found the difference between this and my former state chiefly consisted. I was striving, yea, fighting with all my might under the law, as well as under grace. But then I was sometimes, if not often, conquered; now, I was always conqueror.[4]

The filling of the Spirit was not just an experience; it produced fruit and transformed him.

I remember one of my first experiences of being filled with Holy Spirit. I was 17 years old and after trying to follow Jesus for several years I was exhausted and close to giving up. I attended a youth weekend away and during a time of worship I cried out to Jesus and said, 'Lord, I can't do this any more. If you don't do something I don't think I can keep going. Jesus, please help me.' As I cried out to God, I felt a power surge within me and a love filling my heart. I was overwhelmed and as the youth leaders prayed for me, they prophesied over me and spoke about God's plans and purposes for me. As I talked about this experience with them, they explained that this was the Holy Spirit filling me and empowering me. At that time, I had no understanding of who the Spirit was or his work in a Christian's life. What convinced me that this was God was how different I was. I went to school on the Monday, and I couldn't stop telling my friends about Jesus. I made many mistakes but there was a joy and freedom, and issues that previously overwhelmed me were no longer ruling my life. I then went on to speak in tongues and experience God using me to heal people and set them free from demonic oppression. I could do none of that until the Spirit filled me.

Although separated by centuries, my experience of being filled with the Spirit resonates with Wesley's. First, there is a personal experience of God touching our lives; it can be an experience of peace, love, joy, or heat or power flowing through our body, or a vision or sense of God speaking to us directly or the gift of tongues. No two experiences are the same, but each confirms that God is with us, refreshes us and raises faith. And second, God fills us with his Spirit for a purpose. What God has done in that moment has changed us, given us a gift, released or lifted something from us, begun something new. What marked the Wesleyan revival was his teaching that true Christianity must be evidenced by inward trans-formation and shown by outward signs of transformed life; it was to be experienced. This is the work of the Spirit. It will be people filled and anointed by the Holy Spirit who will transform the Church so that we can be the Church Jesus revives and uses to reveal himself to this nation.

The dregs of Cessationism

You may never have heard of the doctrine of Cessationism, but the churches you and I are part of live with its effects every day of their lives. In essence it is the belief that at the end of the period of the first apostles, when the books of the New Testament were completed, the need for the supernatural gifts of the Holy Spirit (tongues, prophecy, healing and miracles), which were given to confirm the revelation God was bringing through the apostles' teaching and writing, ended. As a result, these gifts of the Holy Spirit 'ceased' after that age and we can no longer expect them to be given to individual believers, even though God may still heal and speak supernaturally as he is free to do.

This belief grew up for some understandable reasons. First, there was a reaction against what was seen as superstition in the Catholic Church around prayers to saints and statues, and miracles that came as a result of these. And second, the reality was that most Christians had never experienced these gifts and there was a need to explain this 'gap' between the current experience and that which they read about in the New Testament. So this doctrine was a logical way to counter these two problems for the Church in the sixteenth century. And it has dominated the Western Church's understanding of the Holy Spirit ever since.

Today there are not many fully signed-up cessationists for several reasons. First, as people have engaged with it, it has become clear that this doctrine has no biblical basis. Second, since the Pentecostal movement began in the 1900s and has spread into other denominations there are so many churches teaching and welcoming these supernatural gifts, it is impossible to argue that the Holy Spirit does not bless his people with these gifts today.

However, although there are not many people who officially adhere to the theory, many Christians in the UK are functional cessationists. They may not deny God's ability to give these gifts to people, but they personally have no experience of them and are a long way off from obeying Paul's instructions to 'eagerly desire gifts of the Spirit' (1 Cor. 14.1). Cessationism is one of those old garments God is asking us to throw out in this reformation rummage sale. And then we have to put on the new clothes he is giving us to wear. The sign that we have put them on will be that the presence and leading and work of the Spirit will be central to the life of our churches rather than an optional extra.

The New Testament presents no other version of the Church and as we now know that the power of the Spirit and his gifts are available to us, there is no justification for not seeking them and allowing them to shape the life of our churches. His work can be expressed through different traditions and forms of worship and there will be a journey for us to grow in it. These are the same miraculous gifts and power of the Holy Spirit that the first Church experienced, and which are experienced by the Church all over the world. He is a supernatural God and the way that he formed the Church was to put his Spirit within his people. God wants a people who are full of him. He wants a deep people who deepen their life in him. It is only deep people, full of the Holy Spirit, who will be able to meet the deep ache of the society around us.

Whether we have experienced the ministry of the Holy Spirit for many years or are only just reading about it now, there is more of God for us to know and experience. There are more of the dregs of the past to throw off and more of the Spirit's life to enter into.

A dependency issue

The legacy of Cessationism is that we have established patterns of church life that depend on other things instead of upon God. So many of the Church's ways reflect the world's ways of leading organizations rather than being the Spirit-filled body of Christ. It is not that our abilities to think and plan and strategize cannot be used in God's service, but they need to be surrendered to Christ. What is the opposite of this dependence on the Holy Spirit? It is a dependency on human ability and control. There are many examples of an intellectualism within our historic denominations that replaces a humble dependence on the Spirit with human pride and ideas. I have been in too many church committees and synods where I witness people's desire to show off their cleverness and so little desire to depend upon God.

The danger is that, in the face of weakness and decline, instead of crying out for resurrection power we take up the tools we are familiar with, such as our institutional levers and strategic business plans, and start to work on the Church. We have seen this in some of the unhealthy approaches of the church growth movement where tools and techniques became the focus. John Drane in his book *The McDonaldization of the Church*[5] warns about franchising the Church as we seek to reform it. In critiquing the evangelical church in the USA with its megachurches Skye Jethani coins the phrase 'the Christian industrial complex',[6] in which a church defines success on the basis of power, numbers and influence and uses mechanistic tools to try to produce this success. Finances and programmes are not the same as spiritual life.

We need a fresh understanding of the Church, free from ambitions for human success. If numbers are the main measure of success in a church then that is what we will be driven to achieve, and it becomes impossible to slow down and pay attention to what God is doing. We become captives on the hamster wheel of producing more and more. Equally as churches we can fear ceasing to exist and start to focus on self-preservation, living with an anxiety about decline and a mindset of scarcity of resources. A church that is determined to preserve its 'life' cannot discover the resources flowing from Jesus' resurrection life. Freedom comes from choosing to stop focusing on numbers and human success and seeking the grace of God and celebrating the signs of what he is doing among us.

Revival

Once we realize God can do the same wonderful works in his Church today as he did in the Church in the book of Acts, we discover a longing for more of God rising within us. Throughout history when this longing has reached a crescendo it has caused people to cry out to God for revival – from the Moravians, to Kenyans, to the Wesleys, to a handful of people in Argentina, to Evan Roberts in Wales, to two elderly sisters in the Scottish Hebrides. Each of these stories of revival has something in common. It began in a desperation for God to move that led a small creative minority of God's people to begin to cry out to him. Although we cannot initiate revival, persistent and prolonged prayer and examination of our lives can raise the sails to catch the wind of heaven when it begins to blow.

It was the same in 1906 in Los Angeles. William Seymour, a black church minister, arrived in Los Angeles and began a prayer meeting in a home with a few other believers. He and other leaders had heard of the Welsh Revival led by Evan Roberts. On the evening of Monday, 9 April 1906, after months of prayer and fasting, Seymour and others at the prayer meeting in Richard and Ruth Asberry's home experienced the Holy Spirit filling them. Spontaneous and passionate prayer for baptism with the Holy Spirit broke out throughout the house. Soon their prayers were answered when Seymour and seven others fell to the floor overcome by the Holy Spirit and began speaking with other tongues as they received the Holy Spirit filling them. The prayer meeting soon outgrew the home where they were meeting and so they moved to an abandoned Methodist church. And as they began to hold services an amazing revival began. From there the Pentecostal movement has spread throughout the world. Today it is the fastest-growing tradition within the Church of Jesus Christ. It is estimated that 13 million people come to faith as part of this movement every year and altogether there are over half a billion members. And the fruit of this is that the Pentecostal convictions of the gifts of the Spirit, miracles and missionary zeal have spread beyond Pentecostalism and birthed charismatic movements in all of the major Christian denominations: Catholics, Anglicans, Baptists and Methodists. I believe God is preparing his Church for a new revival.

A Church that looks like Jesus Christ

The primary work of the Holy Spirit is to glorify Jesus (John 16.14). And so it is the fullness of the Holy Spirit that enables us to be a Church that looks like Jesus: his body on earth. His presence in us by his Holy Spirit is like the DNA in our chromosomes that passes on parents' character traits and physical appearance to their children: the new, *Kainos*, form of who he made us to be. The fruits of the Spirit are the character of Jesus, and the gifts of the Holy Spirit are the ministry of Jesus. We are to look like Jesus. The body of Christ is the image Paul uses in his letters to express this, with every different believer united and directed by Jesus their head, just as in a human body (Eph. 4.15). We see Jesus exercising these gifts: teaching, prophesying, having supernatural knowledge of situations, healing and casting out demonic spirits. How can the Church be his body if we don't conduct his ministry? It astonishes me that we think we can represent Jesus simply with words and with no demonstration of his power and presence.

The Holy Spirit's gifts are the way God has chosen to reveal that he is present and they enable him to act in us and through us. And in 1 Corinthians 12 Paul links the image of the body with each person having at least one of these gifts. Everyone gets to play. On the day of Pentecost Peter testified that God was fulfilling Joel's prophecy that the Spirit would be poured out on everyone and he would speak to his people in powerful ways with dreams and visions and prophecies. And the good news is that he is able to speak so much more clearly and specifically than we ever realized. Once we begin to ask him to guide us and expect to hear his voice we will see the Spirit leading the Church and not human plans. We will see fewer five-year business plans in the Church and yet we will have clearer vision and greater ambition as the Spirit reveals what God is going to do. It will be marked by a simplicity of faith and a quick obedience and willingness to respond to the Spirit's prompting.

The way to engage with the gifts of the Spirit is to eagerly desire them and particularly the gift of tongues. I realize that historically there has been an unhelpful pressure in some Christian traditions for people to speak in tongues. But it is a gift that deepens intimacy with Jesus and opens us to hear God speak and minister in his power. I believe it is significant that this gift was the first gift given to Jesus' followers on the first day of their mission. The start of the church in Ephesus follows the same pattern: Paul prays for the first believers and they speak in tongues and prophesy (Acts 19). He explained that by using tongues we 'utter mysteries by the Spirit' (1 Cor. 14.2) and the Holy Spirit prays through us. The gift of tongues is the most widely given gift of the Holy Spirit to his people and so although no one must speak in tongues and it is not a sign of greater Christian maturity, it is a gift that God gives freely and many of us will need it to strengthen us and deepen our life in God.

I received this gift after reading a book called *Chasing the Dragon*, which describes the missionary work of Jackie Pullinger in a drug- and crime-dominated area of Hong Kong. After Jackie received the gift of tongues, she spent 15 minutes every day praying in the Spirit. As she prayed in tongues she asked God to pray through her and to lead her people. Her testimony was that:

> After about six weeks I noticed something remarkable. Those I talked to about Christ believed . . . This time I was talking about Jesus to people who wanted to hear. I had let God have a hand in my prayers and it produced a direct result. Instead of my deciding what I wanted to do for God and asking His blessing, I was asking Him to do His will through me as I prayed in the language He gave me.[7]

If we recognize the need for personal renewal and strengthening this is a great place to start.

Life in the Spirit

Intimacy with Jesus precedes everything else. Intimacy can feel an intimidating and uncomfortable word. But there is no other word to describe the relationship the Spirit enables us to have with Jesus. Paul describes the Church as the body of Christ (Eph. 4.15) and the bride of Christ (Eph. 5.32) – intimate pictures. Jesus uses the picture of a vine and branches with the life-giving sap of the vine flowing into every branch to describe our life with him, nothing separating us from him (John 15.1–5). We are to live in loving, intimate relationship with Jesus knowing his love for us and responding in love to him. Intimacy with God precedes everything else; everything else flows from this. The form or tradition of a church is not important, but the heart is. It should be overflowing with love for Jesus in the Holy Spirit.

The phrase that I use to describe the presence of the Holy Spirit at work in a church is 'the generative spark'. The difference between churches that have a sense of spiritual life and those that don't is not primarily style; it is the expectation of the work of God among them as they meet together. They expect a generative spark in their midst; as they focus on God's word, sing and pray, receive bread and wine, they go beyond the outward form to seek an encounter with Jesus by his Spirit. This is when transcendence breaks into the immanent frame. This is what transforms us, gives us life, releases joy and puts courage in our veins.

Sadly, the spiritual temperature and the hearts of many of our churches are cold – people held captive by dry ritualism and clericalism that denies faithful Christians the life in all its fullness that Jesus promised us (John 10.10). Such cultures sometimes actively oppose enthusiastic faith and heartfelt expressions of worship and discipleship. Emotional engagement with God is distrusted and patronized. This is the culture that caused those present to criticize the actions of the woman who anointed Jesus' feet with perfume as a waste (Mark 14.4) and Michal to mock her husband King David as he danced before the Lord (2 Sam. 6.16). It is the religious, legalistic spirit that demands control and conformity to the rules of worship and justifies critiquing anything that steps outside that framework as improper or illegal.

And when Jesus spoke to his church in Ephesus through the apostle John he said these words:

Yet I hold this against you: you have forsaken the love you had at first. Consider how far you have fallen! Repent and do the things you did at first. If you do not repent, I will come to you and remove your lampstand from its place. (Rev. 2.4–5)

These are challenging words. Jesus is saying that the first love of overwhelming joy, wonder and gratitude in response to his saving grace must characterize our relationship with him. The implications are hard to face: that he would rather have no church in Ephesus than one that is not passionate in its love for him. There is no version of the Christian faith that the New Testament presents that is not intimately connected with Christ and overflowing with the Holy Spirit. It is not the tradition or form of worship that matters; it is whether it allows for and nurtures a passionate and joyful expression of love for Jesus.

In his book *Movements That Change the World*, Steve Addison explains why this is so important by describing a 'white-hot faith' as the first quality that characterizes such movements:

A white-hot faith is concerned with the Spirit, the Word and the world . . . It calls for consecration of heart, head and hands. Fresh encounters with God through the Word and Spirit energize a missionary movement to go and change the world.[8]

As God calls his Church back to being a missionary movement, this will begin by him setting us on fire by the power of his Spirit.

I am encouraged that there is a growing hunger in ordinary Christians who want to experience the Spirit in their everyday lives and live authentically as followers of Jesus. The restoration of the presence, power and gifts of the Holy Spirit as the source of the Church's life will mark the Church of tomorrow. Why not find some spiritually hungry people you could form a community with, and pray together for the Holy Spirit to fill you and renew you? Ask him to speak and lead you, and pray for God to revive his Church.

Personal response: hunger and thirst

Read: Ephesians 1.17–19.

> I keep asking that the God of our Lord Jesus Christ, the glorious Father, may give you the Spirit of wisdom and revelation, so that you may know him better. I pray that the eyes of your heart may be enlightened in order that you may know the hope to which he has called you, the riches of his glorious inheritance in his holy people, and his incomparably great power for us who believe.

Thank God for the gift of the Holy Spirit and welcome his presence with you.

Pray for yourself what Paul prays in this passage: that you would receive wisdom and revelation from the Holy Spirit and through this would know God better and more intimately.

In light of all the challenges we have addressed in this chapter, remember the hope that we have in Jesus and give thanks.

Pray for the filling and power of the Holy Spirit using the following prayer, which comes from the Church of England's daily prayers between Ascension Day and Pentecost:

> Send your Holy Spirit upon us, and clothe us with power from on high. Blessed are you, creator God, to you be praise and glory for ever. As your Spirit moved over the face of the waters bringing light and life to your creation, pour out your Spirit on us today that we may walk as children of light and by your

grace reveal your presence. Blessed be God, Father, Son and Holy Spirit. Amen.

And now wait quietly for God to answer your prayer.

3

Confident in the gospel

I have but one passion: It is He, it is He alone. The world is the field and the field is the world; and henceforth that country shall be my home where I can be most used in winning souls for Christ.

—Count Zinzendorf

You may never have heard of Dennis the Small, but he influences your life every single day. If it weren't for him, you wouldn't have the birthday you have and you certainly wouldn't be looking forward to Christmas this coming December. Dennis the Small, or to give him his more generous Latin name of Dionysius Exiguus, was a sixth-century monk who lived in what we now know as Eastern Europe. He is credited with the creation of the BC/AD calendar on which all of our dates are based, along with the formula that calculates the dates for Easter. Some 1,600 years after his death, our lives continue to revolve around the chronological framework that he put in place.[1]

For Dennis, time and human history could be divided into two defined periods. There was time before Jesus was born and time after he was born. This was the defining moment around which the story of humankind was centred and his calendar was constructed so that all other events were anchored to the period of time in which Jesus lived on earth. Scholars have debated for many years the accuracy of his calculations, but enshrined in our everyday life is the centrality to human existence of the birth of Jesus.

Paul pre-dated Dennis the Small by some 500 years, but across that time span you can still hear him applauding the work of this faithful monk, whose moniker of 'Small' is actually derived from the Latin for 'humble' rather than a comment on his size. Throughout the letter to the Ephesians, Paul seeks to emphasize the absolute centrality of Jesus' death and resurrection to everything else in their lives and in their world. Just as Dennis decreed that periods of history could be divided up into before and after Jesus, Paul urges the Ephesians to own the truth of this for themselves as individuals. You were dead in your sins, Paul tells them (2.1), but now you're alive in Christ (2.5). You used to follow the ways of the world (2.2), but now you're seated in the heavenly realms with Jesus (2.6). You used to be separate from Christ (2.12), but now you have been brought near (2.13). You were strangers to God and each other, but now you are fellow citizens and members of God's household (2.19). Perhaps summing it all up is verse 5.8, 'For you were once darkness, but now you are light in the Lord.'

And if this is true for the Ephesians and it was true for Dennis the Small, then it is also true for us. All our lives are divided into life without Jesus and life because of Jesus. We all have a BC-JC-AD story. In the words of John Newton, we once were lost, but now are found; were blind, but now we see. It is a before and after story centred on Jesus. It may be that you can't put your finger on a particular moment of decision or definitive conversion. But as you have followed Jesus, you have come to love him and you choose to continue to follow him so that as you reflect on all the events of your life, you can see that they are anchored in the events of his.

In Ephesians 5, Paul is very clear about the natural outworking of having this dynamic in our lives: 'For you were once darkness, but now you are light in the Lord. Live as children of light' (5.8).

Paul states a clear because/so in all his detailing of the difference Jesus has made in their lives. Simply put, all believers have the pleasure/responsibility/blessing/calling/authority to make the light in their lives known to those who don't yet know it for themselves. To let the light of Jesus' presence in them shine. This has always been the core purpose of all church communities: first-century, twenty-first-century and all in between. The Church is primarily a gospel community. We are Jesus' people, an Easter people sharing the good news that Jesus is alive, and death and all that is evil have been defeated.

But in the cultural changes we have referenced and the legacy of a Christendom Church that lost its understanding as a missionary agency, something even more significant happened: we lost confidence in the gospel itself and Jesus' ability to save and transform people's lives. As a result, being intentionally missional, either as individuals or as church communities, has become a massive source of angst and effort rather than a joy and privilege of sharing Jesus with others.

Living out of an alternative story

In the early twentieth century Nikolai Bukharin rose in the ranks of the Russian Communist Party. He was the editor of the Soviet newspaper *Pravda* and was a full member of the Politburo. In 1930 he travelled to Kyiv to address a huge assembly on the subject of atheism. Addressing the crowd he hurled insults, argument and proof against the Christian faith. An hour later he was finished. He looked out at what seemed to be the smouldering ashes of people's faith. 'Are there any questions?' Deafening silence filled the auditorium, but then one man approached the platform and mounted the lectern standing near the communist leader. He shouted the greeting that had been engrained in the hearts and minds of Ukrainian and Russian Christians for centuries: 'CHRIST IS RISEN!' En masse the crowd arose as one, and the response came crashing like the sound of thunder: 'HE IS RISEN INDEED!'[2]

Although we live in a completely different context, twenty-first-century Britain is now also an atheistic, post-Christian culture. And while the attacks are less direct, through media, law-making and education, we are being bombarded daily with a picture of the world in which there is no room for God. So how can our confidence that the gospel still 'works' and saves and transforms people's lives be regained? It is out of our personal encounter with Jesus that we have a living and personal story to tell that reflects *the* story of the gospel. We find our story in his story, and our personal experience of Jesus saving and transforming someone like us reveals that Jesus longs to do that for every single person he has created.

Luke's Gospel tells of how Jesus got into a boat with Peter so he could speak to the crowds and then afterwards he took him out to do some fishing. Peter had been fishing for years, certain that he knew exactly how everything should be working, but it wasn't. Jesus said, 'Put out into deep water, and let down the nets for a catch.' So many fish filled the nets that they nearly broke. Peter's response to this intervention of Jesus was to fall at Jesus' knees and say, 'Go away from me, Lord; I am a sinful man!' And then he pulled up his boat onto the shore and left everything to follow Jesus (Luke 5.4–11). Years later, Peter wrote this in his second letter, verse 1.16: 'For we did not follow cleverly devised stories when we told you about the coming of our Lord Jesus Christ in power, but we were eye-witnesses of his majesty.'

This is where confidence in the gospel comes from, being eyewitnesses to his majesty. To be an eyewitness, you need to see something for yourself that only he can show you, just as only he could simultaneously show Peter a net full of fish and a heart full of sin. This became Peter's story. But then he had to tell others what he had seen. It wasn't easy and he made many mistakes, but this was his 'Dennis the Small' moment: he had seen the power and coming of our Lord Jesus Christ.

Encountering Jesus does not produce indifference. The agnostic uncertainty that marks the faith of many members of our churches exists because we have not enabled them to make Jesus Lord and experience his presence by the Holy Spirit. The way they have been incorporated into church life has not brought them to a personal encounter with Jesus. And because they have not experienced his life-transforming love and power personally, they do not have their before and after story to tell. This has to change.

What is the gospel?

The English word is used to translate the Greek *euangelion*, which means 'a reward for bringing of good news' or the 'good news' itself.[3] And so the gospel is the good news that comes from all that Jesus is, all that he has done and all that he will do. The gospel is the story of Jesus. What we have to offer the world is not a philosophy or set of beliefs but a relationship with the one who is Lord and Saviour of all. Philosopher Ivan Illich said, 'If you want to change a society you have to tell an alternative story.' And we have a better story. In fact the gospel story is THE story that makes sense of our lives, our world, our history and our future. And it isn't just a story about events of the past; it is a living story that becomes our story as we step into it in relationship with Jesus. We live the story and the story continues in and through our lives.

But too often in the past the Church has taken a reductionist approach to the gospel. We have narrowed it and sought to tie it down in neat formulas. As Walter Brueggemann wrote, 'The Gospel is a truth widely held, but a truth greatly reduced. It is a truth that has been flattened, trivialized and rendered inane.'[4] The gospel is the ongoing story of the God-man Jesus who is creator, Lord, Saviour and Judge, who loves this world and everyone in it so much that he gave everything for us. We cannot be satisfied to wear the second-hand clothes of others' theological systems, formulas and statements; we need a personal experience of the good news of Jesus and how wonderful he is, which will overflow in a longing for others to know him.

As we have seen, when Jesus began his ministry he proclaimed the gospel of the kingdom: 'The kingdom of God has come near. Repent and believe the good news!' (Mark 1.15). Jesus came telling a subversive, alternative story about a different kingdom. He was explaining that no longer was the kingdom of God a future event, but in him the opportunity to enter this kingdom had arrived. And as you make him Lord you will experience the love and compassion God has for you and forgiveness of your sins; sicknesses will be healed, evil spirits will be banished, oppression will lift and you will receive life in its fullness for ever. The early Church did not preach the ethic of Jesus, they preached the resurrection of Jesus from the dead. The kingdom is near, because the King is here. And our commission to proclaim the gospel is not to repeat a narrow set of statements, but to be ambassadors of the King and enable people around us to come under his loving reign.

When the first apostles described the gospel they all spoke and wrote about Jesus' life on earth because they were convinced, like Dennis, that this is what had changed the story of the world and has the potential to change every person's story. We cannot separate the good news of the gospel from the events of Jesus' life: his birth, death, resurrection and ascension. It is the gospel of the kingdom, but you can only enter the kingdom through the cross. In the early centuries of the Christian faith the heresies that threatened the Church were all centred around the identity of Jesus. And many brave followers of Jesus fought for the truth of the gospel. Out of their theological battles came creeds that established the key foundational truths of the Christian faith and Jesus' life, such as the Nicene Creed of AD 325.

These truths are under threat again as our culture infects the Church with its rejection of anything absolute or authoritative. Such as with the universalist belief that everyone will go to heaven when they die regardless of whether they have put their faith in Jesus and come into his kingdom. Or the pluralist belief that Jesus is one among many gods who all represent God to us and are of equal value, instead of Jesus being the way, the truth and the life, Lord and creator of all and the only true revelation of God. These threats are based on a devaluation of who Jesus is and the cosmic and eternal significance of his life and death and resurrection. And they cause some Christians to wonder why we should share Jesus with others if believing in him is simply one option among many.

The gospel only makes sense if it is 'the gospel of your salvation' (Eph. 1.13), as Paul calls it. Jesus said that he had come to seek and save the lost (Luke 19.10) and that he would give his life as a ransom for many (Matt. 20.28). The ransom paid by Jesus' death on our behalf addresses the penalty for sin which is death, the right judgement of God, and saves us from eternal separation from God in hell. It is his divine–human blood that achieves our salvation and reconciles us with God. Paul states this twice in Ephesians: 'In him we have redemption through his blood, the forgiveness of sins, in accordance with the riches of God's grace' (1.7) and, 'you who once were far away have been brought near by the blood of Christ' (2.13). And that is why the Church's missionary calling and responsibility to proclaim the gospel is so vital: through our witness people can be saved. This is not socially acceptable language and it makes no sense to our material-istic, immanently framed world. So, it will require thought and care and fresh approaches to show what good news this is to our culture.

Proclaiming the gospel

The Five Marks of Mission are an important statement on Christian mission produced at the Anglican Consultative Council in 1984. They express the Anglican Communion's common commitment to the full gospel of the kingdom rather than a narrow one:

1 To proclaim the Good News of the Kingdom
2 To teach, baptize and nurture new believers

3 To respond to human need by loving service
4 To transform unjust structures of society, to challenge violence of every kind and pursue peace and reconciliation
5 To strive to safeguard the integrity of creation, and sustain and renew the life of the earth.[5]

There is a priority and an order in this mission and, first of all, the Church is called to proclaim the gospel of the kingdom. This then will result in new disciples being made and these new disciples will then love and serve others and work for justice and care for creation. This is the mission of the Church. The mission of God is so much more than Jesus rescuing souls from a lost and broken world, but this is always at its heart. The loving service that the Church offers in communities up and down the country is beautiful and profound and reveals the love of Christ. But the danger that flows from our lack of confidence in the gospel is that the Church will reduce its expression of mission to the last three marks of mission: of loving service, justice and creation care. This is very tempting because these are all things that the world around us affirms and aspires to and none of them require a belief in Jesus. And so this will increasingly become the expression of mission of churches and Christians who choose the future of a compromised mythology. We are already seeing a Church that appears to be more confident in speaking about issues of justice, climate change, politics and economics than it does about Jesus. I am pretty sure that the first apostles had opinions about the oppressive regime of the Roman Empire. But there is nothing recorded about this. They simply took opportunities to share Jesus and kept on doing it even when the authorities tried to silence them. Their proclamation was about Jesus, and this went alongside loving and caring for the poor. It was 'both and' and this is the fullness of the Church's mission that we are called to.

The word 'proclamation' is used to describe sharing the gospel because the original Greek word used for it in the New Testament links to the idea of a herald announcing the victory of a battle. We are to have feet fitted with the readiness of the gospel of peace (Eph. 6.15) to go and proclaim the news of Jesus' victory over sin and death. We have been commissioned as witnesses and heralds. Jesus sent out his 12 apostles and then 72 other followers to represent him and proclaim the gospel of the kingdom and heal the sick. Luke records that he gave them 'power and authority' (Luke 9.1). In creative communities each person knows that they have been commissioned by Jesus and he has given them power and authority to be his representative. They live with a sense of being sent. As the risen Jesus said to his first disciples, "'Peace be with you! As the Father has sent me, I am sending you." And with that he breathed on them and said, "Receive the Holy Spirit"' (John 20.21–22). Wherever we live, in our workplaces, in our families, we have been sent there by Jesus. We are his heralds and ambassadors there. Living with that awareness will sustain us in our mission, and the filling of the Holy Spirit will give us faith that we have been authorized and empowered to do it.

Talking Jesus

However, 'proclamation' can also be an unhelpful term in our context as it conjures up visions of megaphones and shouting loudly. Instead, in a culture that doesn't know Jesus we have to introduce him to people in the way we would a friend. It is an invitational posture to come and meet the person who has transformed our lives. And this is much more conversational. It will involve asking questions and telling stories. Our culture is looking for a message that is authentically lived out by the ones sharing it and so it will involve every one of us sharing Jesus with those around us. Jesus was the divine 'logos', who came and dwelt among us. 'Logos' is translated as 'the word' but it also means the subject of something being discussed.[6] And when Jesus was proclaiming the good news of the kingdom he asked far more questions than he answered and he told stories and had conversations.

A piece of research was conducted in 2022 among 4,000 adults in the UK, called Talking Jesus. This followed up on some equivalent research in 2015 and it produced some fascinating insights.

Of those who were non-Christians, 53 per cent knew someone who was a practising Christian in the UK. But this was a significant drop from the 68 per cent of non-Christians who knew a practising Christian in the UK in 2015. And only 2 per cent of those non-Christians knew a Christian minister. This shows us that we cannot rely on church leaders to do the work of evangelism; it needs to be the whole Church, the whole body of Christ, as we are spread out in society.

Of those asked, 54 per cent believed that Jesus was a real human being, which was a fall from 61 per cent in 2015. But only 16 per cent of those surveyed believed Jesus rose physically from the dead and 24 per cent of people didn't know how to describe Jesus. So, the research reveals the significant missionary task that we have.

But the great news from the research was the experience of non-Christians when a Christian talked about their faith in Jesus: 75 per cent of them felt comfortable with that conversation and 41 per cent felt closer to the Christian who had shared their faith. As a result of it 33 per cent wanted to know more about Jesus, and 36 per cent were open to an experience of encounter with Jesus Christ. That is the headline news of this research: non-Christian people like us talking to them about our faith and it draws many of them closer to Jesus.[7]

I remember leading a mission week to help people build confidence in sharing Jesus with others. We gave people some basic training and then over that week around 100 people visited people's homes nearby and asked them if there was anything we could pray for them. In total 1,500 homes were visited. Around 500 were out when we visited, but of the remaining 1,000 over 500 people let us pray with them. For some it was a simple prayer followed by a thank you and we left. But others experienced God healing them, touching them with his love and peace. Some wanted to hear more and came to faith in Jesus or invited us to come back. No one rejected us aggressively. It was challenging, but it was full of joy, and it released ordinary Christians from the lie that people don't want us to share Jesus with them.

The full gospel

'I want to be well,' said Mohammed and he put his hand on my arm. I had just returned from a mission to Tanzania where we had seen God restore blind people's sight. Someone with a cancerous tumour had been healed, a person who used a crutch to walk threw it away and ran up a hill and a number of people were set free from demonic spirits. A few days after I returned home to Leicester I was chairing the finance committee for the governing body of a local school. They knew that I had been to Tanzania and so they asked me how my trip had gone. In that moment I had a choice as to whether I told them the whole truth. I decided to tell them the whole story. And after I had talked about the water, farming and schools projects we had visited I listed all the miraculous things Jesus had done. They asked me, 'Did that really happen?' and I replied, 'Jesus still does those things today.' And it was then that Mohammed responded in faith. I promised him I would pray for him but the meeting ran on and so he had to leave before it ended. A few days later he rang me and said that he needed to meet with me urgently, and so we arranged to meet in a coffee shop on Market Street in Leicester. The first words that came out of Mohammed's mouth were, 'I need to become a Christian.' He then explained that the moment he had laid his hand on my arm he had felt a peace inside of him that had not gone away. And since that moment he had had none of the pain in his leg that he had been suffering from for three years, which the doctors had been unable to diagnose or treat. Jesus had healed him. And then Jesus saved him in the coffee shop as Mohammed, a Muslim, put his trust in Jesus.

When Paul described his preaching of the gospel in Romans he wrote:

> I will not venture to speak of anything except what Christ has accomplished through me in leading the Gentiles to obey God by what I have said and done – by the power of signs and wonders, through the power of the Spirit of God. So from Jerusalem all the way round to Illyricum, I have fully proclaimed the gospel of Christ. (Rom. 15.18–19)

For Paul, miraculous signs and wonders were an integral part of the gospel. Jesus' ministry was a combination of the proclamation and demonstration of the kingdom breaking in. When Jesus sent out the 72 on mission, he taught them to declare, 'The kingdom of God has come near' and to heal the sick (Luke 10.9).

The biblical pattern is that we must proclaim and demonstrate the gospel. We are to share Jesus and to show Jesus. We show Jesus through loving service and authentic lives that demonstrate the presence of Jesus in our lives and by being agents of the renewal of culture and transformation of local communities. But we also show Jesus through praying and ministering his power and presence with the spiritual gifts God has provided by his Spirit.

It is not just that God is a supernatural God who can only be fully revealed by supernatural signs. But within our culture there is a clear need to demonstrate the reality of God. As Emma Stark wrote, 'spiritual gifts are divine empowerments to operate in the power of God to rescue people'.[8] People are looking for answers to their sense of being lost. They are spiritually seeking in so many different ways and the counterfeit spiritualities that Satan has produced promise tangible spiritual experiences. Through the victory of Jesus Christ and the power of the Spirit people can be healed, set free from evil and experience the loving presence of Jesus. These are signs that cause people to wonder and they shatter the immanent framework that there is no God. Offering prayer in response to someone's needs is something all Christians can do and it is a sign that we care about them and their situation. The gospel is powerful, the most powerful story, and we have to demonstrate it in loving service but also in signs and wonders.

Courageous witnesses

English courts ask witnesses in a criminal case to swear that they will 'tell the truth, the whole truth and nothing but the truth'. We are called to be witnesses to the truth about Jesus. Jesus said, 'you will receive power when the Holy Spirit comes on you; and you will be my witnesses' (Acts 1.8). I hope that as you have read this chapter you have recognized that sharing the gospel is really sharing Jesus and your story of knowing him, inviting others into relationship with him. This is so much more joyful and life giving than preaching and it flows out of our experience of all he is and has done for us. But it won't be easy.

The Greek word for witness is *martus* and from this we derive our English word 'martyr'. Yes, that's right. The call to witness of Jesus Christ became synonymous with being killed for your faith. The early followers of Jesus remained faithful to who they knew Jesus to be, and risked everything, even death, to make him known. And this is the story of the persecuted Church around the world today. I will never forget the evening when I sat in a packed auditorium with 6,000 people at the New Wine summer festival listening to a Christian from North Korea who was there through the support of Open Doors. Liu Son had been arrested and imprisoned in one of North Korea's labour camps. Conditions were cruel and excruciating and deeply uncomfortable to listen to as she described the dead bodies of fellow prisoners left to decompose and be eaten by rats in the corner of her dormitory. The work they had to do was back breaking and it was expected that in the end they would die there.

Yet in that place Liu sustained a life of following Jesus and planted a church. First, she continued to pray and worship. She longed for the days when it would rain because under the cover of the sound of the rain she could sing and worship Jesus. She would take a grain of rice and cup of water and use them symbolically as the body and blood of Jesus and remember him in that act of Holy Communion. And as she came close to him in prayer and worship she sensed that he was calling her to share the gospel with the prisoners around her. This was incredibly dangerous because as soon as she shared with someone she was making herself vulnerable to that prisoner reporting her to the guards and the consequence of that could have been execution. But she would sense the Holy Spirit lead her to a person to focus upon. And as that person went to the toilet, the one place where guards were not present, she would follow them and risk beginning to share the gospel. During the few years she was in the labour camp, she led ten people to the Lord and planted a church.

Liu demonstrated that she understood she had been sent as a witness of Jesus and that the only way her fellow prisoners would hear the good news of Jesus was through her. She lived with that sense of being commissioned and sent by Jesus.

What Liu's story shows is that when we love Jesus and have his compassion for lost people there will be an intent and a determination marking our mission. The problem is that from our Christendom experience we have not developed a courageous faith in which we all understand our calling to share the good news of Jesus with others at whatever cost. The quality of self-forgetfulness that marks the expanding Church around the world and marked the first disciples will need to mark the Church of tomorrow. We will need courage. Courage to speak for Jesus whether it is welcomed or not. Courage to invite those we love to consider following Jesus. Courage to live out our Christian faith in radical ways, even when others within the Church don't join us. Courage to imagine new ways of being church. Courage to offer to pray for the sick. Courage to confront evil and set people free from oppression.

And courage brings joy. It is in having the courage to step forward in some way that we find ourselves depending on Jesus, knowing that only if Jesus shows up does this make sense or have any chance of success. And as we do this, we discover how powerful he is in moments of breakthrough and how faithful he is in the midst of pain and disappointment. Our courage deepens our worship as we bring an offering of sacrificial obedience to him. Playing it safe, living within our means and abilities, means we do not express our faith and there is no adventure in our relationship with Jesus. And our faith withers on the vine and weakens and bears no fruit.

I remember asking the leaders of our missional communities in Leicester, 'How many of you have shared your faith in Jesus with someone in the past year?' And by sharing faith we explained it could be offering to pray, telling a testimony of something Jesus had done, explaining the gospel or responding to a discussion with a Christian perspective. Of the 80 or so people present, less than 20 per cent of them had shared. I went home and wept. I wept because in many ways these were our most committed Christians and so if they weren't sharing Jesus with others, I knew that the rest of the Church wasn't. And I wept because I, as their church leader, had failed to equip them to share Jesus with others.

As we asked them to tell us more about this, we discovered two consistent reasons. First, they were not living with a compassion for the lost nature of people around them and their need to hear the gospel. And second, they didn't know how to share Jesus in ways that felt authentic and that might be received by friends, family or colleagues. We addressed this by teaching in new ways about the good news of the gospel. We encouraged them to engage with their gratitude for all that Jesus had done in their lives. We developed a set of resources to use and trained people in them, such as how to pray every day for five non-Christians and ask God for opportunities to share his love and compassion with them. And we trained them in talking about Jesus and offering prayer to others. Twelve months later we asked the same group of people the same question and over 80 per cent had shared with someone.

Our churches have to equip each disciple to be confident to share Jesus with others, to live out their faith in their everyday lives. I wonder what that might mean in your context.

Personal response: thanksgiving

Read: Ephesians 2.1–5.

> As for you, you were dead in your transgressions and sins, in which you used to live when you followed the ways of this world and of the ruler of the kingdom of the air, the spirit who is now at work in those who are disobedient. All of us also lived among them at one time, gratifying the cravings of our flesh and following its desires and thoughts. Like the rest, we were by nature deserving of wrath. But because of his great love for us, God, who is rich in mercy, made us alive with Christ even when we were dead in transgressions – it is by grace you have been saved.

Take some time to remember your before and after Jesus story: how Jesus has saved you and the difference he has made to your life. Allow a deep gratitude to fill your heart and respond by praising him.

Reflect on the stark description of the need of salvation that Paul gives us here. What challenges you and where is there a need for you to engage again with aspects of the gospel?

Pray for courage and strength to be a witness for Jesus. Ask the Holy Spirit to empower you. My friend Michael Harvey has a simple way to help us engage in this every day and it is an acronym that spells ACORN:

- Ask – 'Lord, is there anyone beyond the church you want me to connect with today?'
- Call – be ready for God to call you to reach out to a particular person.
- Obey – contact them and ask them how they are, do whatever you think is an appropriate sign of God's love and good news.
- Report – share what happened with another Christian and support each other.
- Notice – together discern what God is doing and pray about what to do next.

Have a go at praying like this every day.

4

A disciple-making community

The Church exists for nothing else but to draw men into Christ,
to make them little Christs. If they are not doing that, all the
cathedrals, clergy, missions, sermons, even the Bible itself, are
simply a waste of time. God became Man for no other purpose.
—C. S. Lewis[1]

I was once sitting in a Bishop's Council and discussing this issue of
discipleship. A clergyman who held a senior position in the diocese
became quite frustrated and said, 'Where has all this talk about
discipleship come from? It used to be that all I had to do was take
the service every Sunday, God was on his throne, his people were in
church and then we could all go home. Now I'm expected to disciple
people and it just makes everyone feel guilty.' It wasn't the content
of what he said that shocked me, but the fact that he felt able to say
it publicly, in front of the bishop and his peers, without any fear of
loss of reputation or criticism. That is the culture of many of our
church communities and institutions. And the reason it matters is
that this culture will not equip Christians to make new followers of
Jesus, and any new believers will be inducted into a distorted form
of the Church.

In case we are in any doubt, it was Jesus who commissioned
his followers – not to go to church, but to go and make disciples.
They were to baptize them and teach them to obey everything he
had taught them (Matt. 28.20). And as those first disciples did this
the Church was born. Church is simply the plural of disciple, the
community that is formed by the followers of Jesus. We are to be a
disciple-making community.

By describing the Church in this way we can immediately see the disconnect with how many of us understand the nature and purpose of the Church. In his book *The Great Omission*, Dallas Willard reflects on the complete absence of a lifestyle of discipleship within most churches and the lives of most Christians.[2] Hirsch and Nelson suggest that 'non discipleship might be the single biggest flaw in the Western form of Christianity'.[3] The capacity for our churches to generate authentic followers of Jesus, who will lead others to follow him, is the single most important factor that will determine the effectiveness of the mission of God in our nation. It all stands or falls on this. The credibility of the Church as the representatives of Christ's kingdom is dependent upon the lives of ordinary Christians.

The concept of discipleship comes from the pattern of relationship between a Jewish rabbi and his followers. This was one in which the disciple of the rabbi would seek to learn and obey the teaching of the rabbi but also seek to follow in his ways and imitate his life. Tradition has it that the disciple was to follow the rabbi so closely that the dust from the sole of the rabbi's sandal would fall on the instep of the disciple's foot. Jesus gave those first disciples an experience of discipleship which was a community centred on him, learning to follow him.

The word 'disciple' is another one of those words that we have to re-learn and re-understand. So much of what we have described as discipleship has been birthed in that Christendom cessationist culture. When we hear the word 'disciple' we often think of something like a Bible study or a course or a programme. All of these things are good, but principles and processes must not be substitutes for the presence of Jesus by the Holy Spirit at the centre of creative communities. Jesus' life was one that prioritized presence and people. His disciples watched how he prayed, how he healed the sick and how he loved people. No single interaction was ever the same but all were led by the Holy Spirit. And when they came to do the same in their ministry it was his example that they followed.

And for us, like those first disciples, genuine discipleship comes from knowing Jesus and seeking to follow his ways and his words and allowing him to lead and transform our lives. And what is liberating about this is that our focus does not have to be on changing the Church or solving all its problems. This form of discipleship has a simplicity to it. Our focus is not on systems or targets and outcomes. Instead, it is a devotion to Jesus which will enable his presence in us to begin to shape us and the church communities we are part of.

It's time to die!

I remember going to the Louvre in Paris. We queued to go and view the Mona Lisa. This iconic and enigmatic painting has fascinated people for centuries. What shocked me was what happened when we arrived in front of the painting. As soon as many people in front of us reached that point they stood on the viewing platform and turned their back on the painting. Why? Because they wanted to take a selfie of themselves with the Mona Lisa in the background. Instead of gazing upon its beauty and allowing something of the transcendence contained within it to move them and touch their soul, they wanted to capture the moment and use it to strengthen their reputation as someone who has been to see the painting in the Louvre in Paris. Our postmodern, therapeutic, consumer-focused culture has placed human beings as the centre point of our immanently framed world. And this culture is seeking to disciple us into placing ourselves at the centre of our lives instead of Jesus.

In responding to this all I can say is: IT'S NOT ABOUT YOU! It is all about Jesus and discovering that our best lives are lived in relationship with him and for the purpose of bringing him glory.

And for that to happen we have to die to ourselves and be raised to new life. Our hopes, ambitions, brokenness, pain, attitudes and value systems, loves and relationships, our finances and work – everything has to die. Like the rummage sale that the Church is going through, we each have to clear the space for Jesus to come into and lead our lives. Jesus said to his disciples, 'Whoever wants to be my disciple must deny themselves and take up their cross and follow me. For whoever wants to save their life will lose it, but whoever loses their life for me will find it' (Matt. 16.24–25). The cross is not reserved only for Jesus. The way of the cross is the way of the kingdom. Dietrich Bonhoeffer summarized it thus: 'When Christ calls a man, he bids him come and die.'[4]

This is challenging language. But the problem in our church life and activity is that we are often trying to disciple people before they have died. Discipleship does not work when two competing lives and two competing Lords exist within us: the version of life we are creating and controlling, independently of Jesus; and the one he is calling us to live as our Lord. Too often the Church has presented the process of a person becoming a Christian as joining the Church and adding Jesus to their team. Jesus is expected to affirm who they are and what they do, to like the things they like, agree with their opinions, and reject and condemn whatever offends them. They have gained a heavenly supporters' club of the Holy Trinity and the angels. This is consumer Christianity but it's not discipleship. Dying to self is never portrayed in Scripture as something optional in the Christian life. It is the reality of the new birth; no one can come to Christ unless they are willing to see their old life crucified with Christ and begin to live in obedience to him.

A couple of centuries ago, a band of brave souls became known as one-way missionaries. They purchased one-way tickets to the mission field. Instead of suitcases, they packed their belongings into coffins. As they sailed out of port, they waved goodbye to everyone they loved, knowing they would never return home. A. W. Milne was one of those missionaries. He set sail for the New Hebrides in the South Pacific, knowing full well that the local inhabitants had martyred every missionary before him. His coffin was packed. He was warned on the boat not to go there because he was likely to die. And his reply was, 'I died a long while ago.' For 35 years, he lived among the tribes and loved them. When he did die, tribe members buried him in the middle of their village and inscribed this epitaph on his tombstone: 'When he came there was no light. When he left there was no darkness.'[5]

Start as you mean to go on

Start as you mean to go on is a good principle in life and one that the Church would do well to pay attention to. And it brings us to the word 'baptize' within Jesus' Great Commission. Sacraments of baptism and Holy Communion are vital aspects of every church community because they retell the story of Jesus again and again, they unite us with Christ in his death and resurrection, and they enable us to receive his grace, his life-giving empowering presence. The commandment from that Great Commission is first to *make* a new disciple, then *mark* them with baptism, and then *mature* them by teaching them to obey everything Jesus commanded you.

I have often wondered what the consequences have been of the practice of many historic denominations in our country to baptize babies of parents with no active faith in Christ; another hangover from Christendom. It isn't that I am against children being baptized; it's just that the separation of the act of baptism from faith undermines the power of baptism. In Christian baptism, being immersed in the water symbolizes dying and being buried with Christ (Rom. 6.4–8) and coming out of the water pictures Christ's resurrection. Being fully submerged under the water is literally the meaning of the Greek word *baptizō*; it was used to describe washing dishes, and shipwrecks.[6] Many churches and members have only seen the sprinkling of babies. Both of my children were baptized as babies by full immersion, one in a baptistry and one in a storage container filled with water, to try to communicate the full meaning of this sacrament. Sprinkling communicates the cleansing work of Christ but loses the submission and death to self and rising to new life that baptism represents.

Recently I witnessed the baptism of a man who had no earthly goods but was determined to take off one set of clothes, be baptized and then put on a new set, leaving the old ones behind. Even though he couldn't afford to give up any of his clothes he would not take the old set back. He was determined to leave the old self dead and buried in the waters. In the Church of tomorrow, as we see thousands of adults come to faith in Christ, I believe we will see immersion baptism as normal, alongside the baptism of children of believing parents. It is symbolic but it is also spiritually powerful. As people are baptized in this way they can experience deliverance from evil, the breaking of patterns of sin, washing away of shame and being filled with the Holy Spirit. Then they are ready to be disciples of Jesus.

Jesus' love language is obedience

The test or sign of whether we have died to ourselves and are living for Jesus is our willingness to obey him. We have already heard that following baptism the next part of Jesus' discipleship process is learning to obey him. Obedience is not an easy word or a word that settles naturally in us in our culture, but it is at the heart of discipleship. The concept of love languages helps those of us who are married to understand that the way we express our love for our husband or wife may not actually be the way that they feel most loved. For example, it has been a marriage-saver for me to know that emptying the dishwasher is a much greater demonstration of my love for my wife Bridget than buying her flowers, because her love language is acts of service. Though it's not one of the five love languages described in Gary Chapman's famous book on this subject,[7] we need to understand that obedience is Jesus' love language. We can only claim to love Jesus if we desire to obey him. Jesus teaches his disciples in that upper room discourse, 'If you love me, keep my commands' (John 14.15) and, 'If you keep my commands, you will remain in my love' (John 15.10). He couldn't have been clearer.

Reframing obedience within an understanding of love and relationship is vital. Otherwise, it portrays Jesus as a Lord who is demanding and unreasonable. Nothing could be further from the truth. Obeying Jesus deepens our trust and brings us closer to him. And it doesn't shut down the conversation; it stimulates it. The disciples were constantly asking Jesus questions about things they didn't understand or that weren't working. As we try to work out what obedience means for us in a situation, we can wrestle with God through his word and in prayer. And we are not doing it in isolation – we are doing it with other disciples. Together we love and support one another as we seek to follow Jesus. We are there to pick each other up when we get it wrong, we stand together in the midst of pain and we challenge one another to follow Jesus. This is what Church is for. And every little decision to obey Jesus releases a fresh work of grace to become more like him by the Holy Spirit.

Dietrich Bonhoeffer was calling the Church in his day back to being a creative minority living in obedience to Christ. He was living in Germany as a Lutheran Church pastor at a time when the Nazi regime was rising and the Church was weak and compromised. In response he wrote the book *The Cost of Discipleship* in which he spells out what he believes it means to follow Christ. Within it he writes:

Discipleship means adherence to Christ, and, because Christ is the object of that adherence, it must take the form of discipleship. An abstract Christology, a doctrinal system, a general religious knowledge on the subject of grace or on the forgiveness of sins, render discipleship superfluous, and in fact they positively exclude any idea of discipleship whatever, and are essentially inimical to the whole conception of following Christ. With an abstract idea, it is possible to enter into a relation of formal knowledge, to become enthusiastic about it, and perhaps even to put it into practice but it can never be followed in personal obedience. Christianity without the living Christ is inevitably Christianity without discipleship, and Christianity without discipleship is always Christianity without Christ.[8]

We learn through obedience

The literal meaning of the word 'disciple' is 'learner'.[9] The nearest equivalent in our culture is 'apprentice'. An apprentice is someone who works for a skilled or qualified person in order to learn a trade or profession or new skill. We imagine a young apprentice learning the skills of carpentry or plumbing from an experienced and qualified practitioner. She is first of all looking at how he performs different tasks. She waits for opportunities to do aspects of the job herself because the whole purpose of this work is for her to become like him, able to do that work. She listens to instructions from him and follows his guidance on how to do it. And she practises the new skill. This model, which has been summarized as 'I do – you watch', 'you do – I help', 'you do – I watch', is the process Jesus took his disciples through. He apprenticed them as disciples who announced and demonstrated the kingdom and made disciples; they learned the skills of making disciples.

Teaching disciples the Christian faith is the responsibility of every church. But in many churches people are not expected to make any change as a result of the teaching they receive and then they come back the next week and learn another lesson, which they also fail to apply. No one asks anyone how they are getting on following Jesus. And over the years we subconsciously conclude that following Jesus is about learning information and affirming our faith in him in public worship, instead of allowing him to transform every area of our life as we obey him. We have a distorted version of Christian maturity which equates with knowledge accumulation instead of actively following Jesus. As Mark Batterson said in a talk I attended, 'We have been educated beyond the level of our obedience.'

There are three aspects of the disciple's apprenticeship process: information, imitation and incarnation. Information is important; we need to understand Jesus' teaching. Second, we then need other more experienced Christians to be examples and give support in how to apply this to our lives. Having their example to imitate is why Jesus has put us together in the Church. As Paul wrote, 'I urge you to imitate me' (1 Cor. 4.16) and, 'Follow my example, as I follow the example of Christ' (1 Cor. 11.1). And finally, we have to take responsibility for incarnating that truth authentically in our lives, working out what it means in our context. My friend Paul Blackham gives a great example of this process. As people come to faith he takes them on a journey of reading Jesus' teaching from the Sermon on the Mount and helping them to begin to put it into practice. Each week he meets with the new believers and asks them how they got on living out the lesson they learned the previous week. For instance, if they read Jesus' commandment to love their enemies (Matt. 5) and they hadn't managed to do that with someone they needed to forgive at work, Paul talks it through with them and helps them to overcome whatever is difficult. He explained to me that the reason this is so important is if they haven't put it into practice, they will not discover how life giving and transformative following Jesus is. But when they do manage to obey Jesus, they now have a testimony of how he has changed their life, they won't want to live any other way, and they want to tell everyone else they know about it.

Patterns not programmes

Bonhoeffer's expression of a creative minority was to create a discipleship training school at a place called Finkenwalde. Some of his friends were concerned that what he was doing was too extreme or overly spiritual. Wilhelm Niesel came to visit him and Bonhoeffer took him on a trip up a hill, from which they could see a large field in the distance. There a squadron of German fighter planes were taking off and landing, and hundreds of soldiers were moving and practising their drills. Bonhoeffer spoke of a new generation of Nazis in training, whose disciplines were formed 'for a kingdom . . . of hardness and cruelty'. It would be necessary, he explained, to develop a superior discipline if the Nazis were to be defeated: 'You have to be stronger than these tormentors that you find everywhere today.'[10]

The culture around us wants to disciple us. It wants to teach us its ways and calls us to believe its truths. The devil is called 'the ruler of the kingdom of the air' (Eph. 2.2). He is the one leading this culture with false promises. We need a discipleship culture and practice that is stronger than the world of philosophers, marketing agencies, social media influencers, advertisers and campaigners. They all want our devotion, calling us to 'sign up', 'follow', 'like' their vision of this world. Obedience to Jesus implies disobedience towards other competing lords and idols.

And these patterns of discipleship need to be developed in community and not as programmes or courses. It's not that training materials and courses of teaching are not useful but they in themselves do not forge disciples. What's needed are deep relationships centred around Jesus and patterns of life that enable us to follow him. The heart cry of members of our churches today is that they don't want to be cogs in an organizational church machine; they want to live a life in which they flourish following Jesus. And so the rhythms and patterns of community life need to be authentic and organic rather than mechanistic. Much more like a gardener tending a vine to grow Christlikeness in us.

The only context for disciple-making is community. Jesus' example was to form a small group of 12. This was the first church. As someone has said, 'Carrots grow in rows, disciples grow in circles.' It is in these small creative communities that we can grow as we share life with one another. The Sunday service sitting in rows has its place, but it will not produce life-transforming relationships. Form must follow function. The purpose of what is being made determines its shape and size so that it is as effective as possible. The purpose of the Church is to make disciples who will make disciples. We need new forms of community centred on Jesus which prioritize his presence among his people and obeying his word.

Discipleship does, as the roots of the word suggest, require discipline. These discipleship patterns are necessary to create habits in our lives that shape us for God's kingdom. Dallas Willard says that these discipleship disciplines:

> are activities of mind and body purposefully undertaken, to bring our personality and total being into effective cooperation with the divine order. They enable us more and more to live in a power that is, strictly speaking, beyond us, deriving from the spiritual realm itself.[11]

Like Willard, Wesley knew that Sunday worship alone was not enough to produce fruit and growth in people's lives. He organized people into three interconnected discipleship groups called Societies, Classes and Bands. People came together to pursue a deeper faith in these different groups with different sizes and purposes. Societies were the largest groups with an average of 50 or more people, where people could invite friends and they came together to learn more about Methodism and grow in faith. They included preaching, teaching, Bible reading and hymn singing. Class meetings were in effect home churches with 12 members and a designated leader. They met weekly for prayer, instruction and mutual fellowship. The weekly Class meeting involved each member giving a report on their spiritual progress and needs and receiving prayer and support from the group. Wesley's famous question was, 'How is it with your soul?'[12] Wesley encouraged those who attended Societies and Classes to be involved in smaller Band meetings as well. These were for encouragement and accountability. The Band was smaller than a Class and had more rigorous requirements. It was divided by gender and was to be a place where the members of the group could confess their sins and receive prayer. There were specific questions which the members asked of one another about sin and their determination to avoid it.

It can seem impossible to imagine how people would submit their lives to such accountability and there are challenges around doing this in a healthy way. But what I want us to note is how this was all based on the expectation that being a follower of Jesus involved spiritual passion and desire for growth in Christlikeness and commitment to obeying him. One of the changes we are realizing must happen in our church life is that we need to raise the bar on what it means to be a disciple and lower the bar on what church is and who can lead it. More on the second half of that statement later, but raising the bar on living as a disciple is crucial. It will mean sharing our lives with others, in open, accountable relationships that will be the new normal. Each disciple will call others to a deeper devotion to Christ. And such relationships allow creative communities to form and be filled and shaped by the Holy Spirit.

I want to finish this chapter with a tangible example of what this can look like. Around the world and around the UK, people are finding that a structure of small community gatherings divided into 'three thirds' is a helpful trellis to support the growth of these communities. As people meet they focus on doing three things together.

They look back. They share how their week has gone, open their lives to one another. They give testimony of what God has been doing in their lives. As part of this they ask one another questions of accountability about how they got on doing what they said they were going to do in obedience to Jesus last time they met.

They look up. They pray and worship passionately. They read Scripture and listen to what Jesus is calling them to do.

They look out. They talk about what they are going to do as a result of what God has said to them and they discuss and pray for their lives and missionary work.

And when they focus on God's word they use a tool called Discovery Bible Study (DBS) which is used by many church-planting movements. DBS involves reading a passage of Scripture and then asking someone to retell that passage in their own words to help people engage with it. Then they ask four simple questions:

- What does this story tell me about God?
- What does it tell me about human life?
- If this really is God's word, what will I do in response to it?
- Who am I going to tell about what I have learned from this?

The simplicity of these questions is the key. They depend on the power of God's word and on the Holy Spirit; they are not clever enough to work without him and they have a laser focus on obeying what God has said to us. Simplicity leads to reproducibility as it also means that anyone can now lead a small church community gathered in a home following this pattern; it releases people into leadership. But the most important reason why they are simple is because they are also the way that people can lead others to faith in Jesus. Inviting people to come together and read gospel stories about Jesus and then asking these questions is an incredibly effective way of enabling them to encounter Jesus. It builds relationship and shared lives with Jesus at the centre of them from the beginning. Those who participate are becoming disciples even before they have believed. We are seeing new church communities form out of people coming to faith in this way.

Dave was a friend of mine whom I had met through his wife who was a Christian. He was a highly respected professor at a university and a gifted musician and sportsman. One day when we met for a coffee, I shared my story of coming to faith in Jesus. He was moved by this and shared that he wanted to experience it for himself. We met over the next few weeks and read gospel stories using the DBS questions. One week we read the story of the unmerciful servant and Jesus' call to forgive others. Dave said, 'I know what you're going to ask me,' and he listed the questions to me. So, I said he could lead the session, and he did and shared his need to forgive people who had opposed him at work. He chose to obey Jesus' command that week, and encountered Jesus and came to faith in him. Because Dave knew the pattern of using these questions to read a story together and how powerful it can be, he then went on to lead a new church community using this DBS tool and he led a number of new people to follow Jesus. It was the simplicity of the tool that enabled Dave to be a disciple who made disciples from the start of his journey with Jesus.

As we consider all the ways in which our understanding and practice of discipleship will need to change over time, we need to think of how new communities that embody these values can begin to form and make new disciples. Where and how might God be calling you to be involved in this?

Personal response: discipline

Read: Ephesians 4.15–16.

> Instead, speaking the truth in love, we will grow to become in every respect the mature body of him who is the head, that is, Christ. From him the whole body, joined and held together by

every supporting ligament, grows and builds itself up in love,
as each part does its work.

Take the DBS questions from this chapter and use them to reflect
on this passage.

Reflect on how you can 'incarnate' and apply any of the examples
given in this chapter to your context and pray for God to enable you
to be obedient to his calling.

As we have talked of Wesley in this chapter, finish by praying
John Wesley's Covenant Prayer:

I am no longer my own, but yours.
Put me to what you will, place me with whom you will.
Put me to doing, put me to suffering.
Let me be put to work for you or set aside for you,
Praised for you or criticized for you.
Let me be full, let me be empty.
Let me have all things, let me have nothing.
I freely and fully surrender all things
To your glory and service.
And now, O wonderful and holy God,
Creator, Redeemer, and Sustainer,
You are mine, and I am yours.
So be it.
And the covenant which I have made on earth,
Let it also be made in heaven.
Amen.[13]

5

Churches that plant churches

The single most effective evangelistic methodology under heaven is planting new churches.

—Peter Wagner[1]

The Church was created as a movement. As we read the book of Acts we see the Church as an organic grassroots missionary movement spread out before our eyes. The Church grew as the Holy Spirit inspired men and women to share their faith and new churches were formed. Wherever they went, whether on mission, or as they travelled, or were scattered because of persecution, the gospel spread and people gathered together to follow Jesus in new churches. These churches were in the homes of ordinary people. It was an unstoppable movement that was sustained by new churches planting churches again and again.

In many places around the world the Church still is this missionary church-planting movement. I remember standing on a road that ran northwards in Uttar Pradesh in northern India. With me was the priest of an indigenous Indian church who had been tasked with evangelizing a region where millions of people who had never heard the good news of Jesus lived. The road stretched 100 miles ahead of us and he explained his strategy. 'We will go to a village and share the gospel and keep sharing until someone comes to faith in Christ. When that happens we will start an informal church with those new believers and help them share their faith. We will seek to serve the needs of the local community and establish a permanent church. Once this has happened we will ask someone from that new church to go to the next village and do the same. We will do this in every village a mile either side of this road until we reach the end of the road.'

But in the UK the Church stopped being this missionary church-planting movement many generations ago. David Garrison, who studies church-planting movements around the world, defines them as 'a rapid multiplication of indigenous churches planting churches that sweeps through a people group or population segment'.[2] And he reveals that against his definition there is no such movement in a Western context. And so we arrive at another aspect of the Christendom cataract: the static nature of the Western Church. The cultures over which Christendom presided have no examples of church-planting movements. Our current form of church is perfectly designed to produce the results it is producing, and it is no accident that the historic denominations are in decline; they have been established for maintenance not mission. So, although I am really encouraged that within the UK a wonderful variety of new churches are being planted by every denomination, this is currently embryonic and slow and those maintenance systems often defend themselves against this movement. The sobering conclusion I draw from this is that when the Church stops being a movement it actually stops fully being the Church. And if what we have been doing in the recent past has not produced movement, we need to make significant changes in order to look something like Jesus' intention for his Church.

The church you are a member of was planted once. I wonder if you know its story. Someone in the past had a vision to create a place and a people where God is worshipped and glorified, and others can come to know Jesus Christ. That vision resulted in your church being established and you having a community of believers to belong to. It can be really encouraging to research the story and use it as inspiration for your mission today. The only problem is that, for many, the story has probably paused there. I say 'paused' because God hasn't finished yet and in Christ your church has the potential to reproduce and plant a new church and, together with that new congregation, to go on to plant other churches.

Church-planting language captures the understanding of organic Spirit-led multiplication. The Bible speaks of sowing and reaping (John 4.37; 2 Cor. 9.6), planting and watering (1 Cor. 3.6), growing (Matt. 13; 1 Pet. 2.2; 2 Pet. 3.18) and bearing fruit (Matt. 7.17–20; John 15.1–16; Gal. 5.22). And the Bible also uses the metaphor of a body that is living and growing to describe the Church (1 Cor. 12.12–27; Eph. 4). The Church is a spiritual organic plant that the Father is tending and nurturing and it is the living body of Christ on earth. And our churches are supposed to multiply.

New wineskins?

Jesus said, 'Neither do people pour new wine into old wineskins. If they do, the skins will burst; the wine will run out, and the wine-skins will be ruined. No, they pour new wine into new wineskins, and both are preserved' (Matt. 9.17).

Jesus was talking about the renewed people, with new relation-ships, attitudes and life of the kingdom that he was inaugurating. And he was saying that it would be destructive if God poured out his Holy Spirit into people and communities and structures that were not ready for this; it would tear them apart. Jesus' solution was to say that he would create new, *kainos*, wineskins to hold the new wine and leave the old wineskins to hold the old wine. Jesus is using the genius of the 'both and' approach instead of 'either or' and it ensures nothing good is lost.

This is such a helpful parable for us as we consider the Church of tomorrow. First, if God is preparing his Church for a fresh pouring out of his revival power then we have to be ready; there is a need for new wineskins that will not resist this move and will be prepared and ready to move with him. The implication is that, without this,

God will not pour out his Spirit in this way because there are not churches ready to receive this new power.

But it also gives us an understanding that the new and the old can coexist and the new forms alongside the old. The Mixed Ecology analogy of the Church of England is founded on this principle: that there are many different plants in the ecology of a garden and different plants grow best in different places. So, it is not a one-size-fits-all approach, but instead we believe God as the gardener wants to see many different types of plant grow and flourish. Healthy parish churches can continue their ministry and enable new church communities to form in their parishes and work in partnership.

But the danger comes when the old prevents the new from forming. The reason why the new has to come is because the old understanding of church and its structures focused on maintenance will not enable the Church to become the missionary movement we are called to be. An interesting aside is that the reason wine was put in wineskins rather than bottles is that these would travel better, sitting easily against the side of a donkey or camel, and were not easily broken. The wineskin enabled movement because of its flexibility. The inflexibility of our current forms of church is a significant challenge today.

What is the Church?

This is perhaps the most foundational question of this book. What is the Church? The New Testament Greek word that is translated 'church' in our English Bibles is *ekklēsia*. Understanding the meaning of *ekklēsia* is vital to understanding the nature of the Church. This Greek word appears in the New Testament 115 times and in every instance, except three, it is translated as 'church'.[3] For example, Acts 11.26 says that 'Barnabas and Saul met with the church [*ekklēsia*] . . . at Antioch'.

The three exceptions where this word is not translated 'church' are found in Acts 19.32, 39 and 41 where Paul and his team are on mission in Ephesus. In these three cases the translators use the word 'assembly' instead of 'church', because in Acts 19 it is describing the assembly of merchants and city elders who gathered to complain about what Paul and his team had been saying about Jesus and the local belief in the god Artemis. The word *ekklēsia* literally means 'the called-out ones' (*ekk* = out + *kaleo* = call). So this word was used in Greek to describe a civil body of selected people. It was used generally to describe an assembly brought together for decision-making purposes and it was specifically used to describe a local town council: a civil governing body. And this was the word the Holy Spirit inspired the Gospel writers and the first apostles to use to describe the Church. This is very significant because it expresses that the Church was a body of Christians distinct and called out from the world they were in, coming together into a separate assembly under no king but Jesus. And they had now been appointed by him to exercise authority in his name to bring his loving rule to bear in this world and see people saved and communities transformed. I wonder how you would describe what a local church is.

From that understanding of *ekklēsia* my working definition of church is this:

a community of disciples with Jesus at its centre, seeking to obey him and see his kingdom come in this world.

When our understanding of church is expressed in these simple basic requirements we are liberated to imagine how it can be expressed in new ways. Jesus said, 'For where two or three gather in my name, there am I with them' (Matt. 18.20). He is affirming the simplicity that when two or three of his followers meet in his name, accepting his authority and being centred on him, he will be with them. This is Jesus' definition of church. There is a sense at this time that Jesus is inviting us to be ecclesiologists and to discern together what he is calling his Church to be and do.

Why plant new churches?

A recent survey for the National Churches Trust revealed that there are around 40,000 church buildings in the UK.[4] And when church planting is mentioned people will often say that we already have plenty of churches that have lots of room; let's work on filling them up before we start any new ones. Alongside this is the reality that the churchgoing population is currently a shrinking pie and so any new church will just take people from churches that are already declining and will weaken everyone. So people ask, 'Shouldn't we first help the churches that are struggling by investing more resources there?' So, the 'why?' of church planting needs to be answered.

New churches reach new people

Church planting is not an end in itself. We embark on the adventure of forming a new community for the single purpose of enabling lost people to be reconciled to God and have a home in his kingdom. New churches are shaped by the missionary purpose of connecting with different people. All the studies of church plants in the UK have shown that newly planted churches have a higher percentage of people involved who did not previously belong to a church.

We have to be brave enough to ask the honest question: who isn't here? Who and what type of people have no connection with our church? Who isn't gathering with us to worship Jesus? The answer will often be those of younger generations, but it might also be that there are very few men in the congregation, or people from different ethnic backgrounds from our local community are missing, or there is no one from a certain local geographical area.

And then we have to ask: what are we going to do about this? My experience of churches up and down the country is that they are made up of lovely, faithful Christian people. And they have an established pattern of worship that is precious to them and has nurtured their faith over many decades. The amount of change that would be required for this pattern of worship to connect with those missing generations and communities would seem, in my opinion, unnecessary and ineffective. Instead, by forming a new church community we can start something new alongside established congregations. The existing church supports that new venture as they pray and give financially and as some people join the new team to plant a new congregation. This 'both and' approach resolves the tension between caring for and nurturing the existing congregation and at the same time seeking to reach new people with the gospel.

Mission with rather than mission to

When we get close to people our mission changes from doing things 'to' people or 'for' people to doing things 'with' people. We move from trying to attract people to come to where *we* are and instead we 'go', as Jesus commanded us, to be with people and form church where *they* are. This reflects the incarnational principle of God's mission in Jesus. Missionary organizations often talk about the call to go to unreached people groups around the world where there is currently no church. But every single one of us lives in an under-reached place where there are not enough church communities connecting with different people who don't know Jesus. Today those ends of the earth that Jesus spoke of may well be at the end of your street.

When we move to join people where they are on their journey, hospitality becomes the place where community begins to form. Sharing food and sitting together enables us to listen and learn. It's the place where we hear the stories people tell about themselves and their lives. Church planting always begins with listening to God and his heart for a place or people, listening to the people and listening to the land, to the history and current situation of that place. And as we listen to these voices it is the place where we can tell the story of Jesus and our experience of him, help people to see that it can be their story and invite them to join us – just as Jesus told the 72 disciples he sent out on mission to accept invitations into people's homes, and within that place of hospitality to heal the sick and declare that the kingdom of God is here (Luke 10). Then church forms out of those relationships in a deep and profound way that reflects the love of God for that community.

Proximity matters because it makes the Church visible to people. Not the visibility of a church building but a loving community. Jesus gave this command to his disciples: 'A new command I give you: love one another. As I have loved you, so you must love one another. By this everyone will know that you are my disciples, if you love one another' (John 13.34–35). Jesus says people will notice the quality of love that his followers have for one another. This is why we plant churches, to get close to where people are in each neighbourhood, workplace, gym, school, the places people gather together; to be creative minorities living in such a loving way that people start to wonder what is going on. As Will Willimon wrote:

> The most eloquent testimony of the resurrection is not an empty tomb or a well-orchestrated pageant on Easter Sunday but rather a group of people whose life together is so radically different, so completely changed from the way the world builds community that there can be no explanation other than that something decisive has happened in history.[5]

I mentioned Fiona earlier. She planted a new church on the Haywoods Village new housing estate near Weston-super-Mare. It came out of a growing compassion that God gave her for the people on that estate five minutes from where she lived. She started to walk her dog on the estate, became a school governor and joined the WI. As she listened to the people she saw a need to build community, and so with the help of her local church she started a pop-up café in the local school once a week. This built friendships between people and when Fiona invited some of them to an Alpha course they came. From this a tea and toast church has formed and a midweek missional community. All of this started while Fiona was working as a financial advisor. She simply listened and as she began to sense God's heart for people in that community, she obeyed, and a church was born.

Church planting renews the Church

New churches do things in completely new ways as they experiment and allow their context and mission to shape them. And these ideas and new forms of church don't stay within those churches; they present a fresh picture of what is possible to established churches. Again, we have seen this happening in so many ways with fresh expressions of church: Forest Church, Wrestling Church, Muddy Church, sports-based churches, Messy Vintage Church, Café Church. Each one of these has a unique connecting point with people, and forms church around their needs and interests, and the creativity that has been released through these new forms of church is filtering into the wider Church. And as churches plant churches which go on to plant other churches, new networks will grow and these networks will begin to reveal new life-giving patterns of relationship between churches to sustain church-planting movements.

Ultimately, if our nation is to be evangelized again we will need a saturation of churches so that everyone has a church close enough to reach them. We will need a diversity of churches to reach different types of people. And we will need these churches to be Spirit-filled disciple-making communities that can lead people to faith in Jesus. We have a big challenge ahead of us, but I'm so encouraged that we are seeing the first shoots of all of this.

Organic and organized

The church in Ephesus was a church-planting church. We read in Acts 19.9–10:

> So Paul . . . took the disciples with him and had discussions daily in the lecture hall of Tyrannus. This went on for two years, so that all the Jews and Greeks who lived in the province of Asia heard the word of the Lord.

The question we have to ask is: how did the whole population of Asia (southern Turkey today) hear the word of the Lord? We can't imagine them all arriving at midday in the Hall of Tyrannus in Ephesus when Paul was doing his training. The only explanation is that the disciples whom Paul trained in those sessions over two years went out on mission and planted churches. And we know that they did because the names of the churches that Jesus addresses in Revelation 2 and 3 are all local towns around Ephesus as well as Ephesus itself. Those disciples went out from Ephesus with the gospel, saw people come to faith and planted new churches, so that there were enough to give everyone in Asia a chance to hear the gospel.

This is such a great example of how church planting happens as the gospel spreads and how those churches then further spread the gospel. And it is also an example of the organization that accompanies this organic growth. Paul first of all plants what the Church of England would call a Resource Church in the urban centre of that region and establishes a training centre from which to send missionaries. These missionaries then plant new churches in the homes of people in the town or village where they have been sent. Every now and again in the New Testament we read of the homes where churches were based: Mary's house church (Acts 12.12), Lydia's house church in Philippi (Acts 16.40), Priscilla and Aquila's house church (Rom. 16.3, 5), Nympha's house church (Col. 4.15) and Philemon and Apphia's house church (Philem. 1-2).

In the UK there is a need for all kinds of churches to fulfil different aspects of the mission of God. Resourcing church centres create strong ministries, often reaching a younger genera- tion of people, and can church plant across a region. Sending teams to revitalize a church within a church building that has declined is a vital strategy as church buildings continue to be places of connection and loving service to communities. And planting new church communities focused on reaching certain people with teams of two to ten is agile and responsive to what God is doing and opportunities that develop. As my friend Christian Selvaratnam says, just as Tesco has Tesco Extra, Tesco Superstores, Tesco Metro, Tesco Local and even garage fore- courts, so the Church needs to understand the different roles and types of church and sizes of church that are needed. Just as it was for Paul, it is an organic process that requires investment and organization.

Myriad

Myriad is an initiative to serve the Mixed Ecology vision of the Church of England to see thousands of new worshipping communities form. And we want to inspire similar growth in other church denominations and networks. We formed Myriad in response to the sense of urgency to reach our nation with the gospel, asking what pattern of church and church life was needed to achieve this. It was this approach that caused us to wonder if we could see many new church communities planted, led by laypeople and without the restrictions of buildings and salaries. This is what we see around the world today and in Church history. And the key to this is these communities are small and have a very simple life. All of Jesus' parables about the multiplication of his kingdom begin with the smallest seed. Simple things are reproducible.

The small church communities are sometimes called micro churches, house churches, ecclesial communities. They can meet anywhere because not only is the Church not the building, it does not always need its own building. They allow multiplication and movement because ordinary Christians can lead them equipped with the Holy Spirit and Scripture. And because of their size, these church communities can be families. I am convinced that extended family is a key pattern for the new churches God is forming in our nation. Churches where we love one another and share resources, eat and have fun together, share lives and help each other grow. These extended families on mission together are the creative communities Jesus is planting to reach new people.

But although this is simple, there is so much unlearning and new understanding that needs to take place, we think this requires investment of resources and thinking. Rather than encouraging a reckless have-a-go attitude, Myriad offers to be a catalyst for change, thought partners and travelling companions through the resources we are developing, the training pathway we offer.

Roland Allen was a twentieth-century Anglican priest, missionary and missiologist. He studied the early Church and the missionary methods of Paul and compared them to the Church in his day. He wrote in his book *The Spontaneous Expansion of the Church* that if our strategy can't attain what Jesus commanded us to do, then we ought to change our strategy. And later in that book he wrote this:

The spontaneous expansion of the Church reduced to its elements is a very simple thing. It asks for no elaborate organisation, no large finances and no great numbers of paid missionaries . . . The organisation of a little Church on the apostolic model is also extremely simple and the illiterate converts can use it and the poorest are sufficiently wealthy to maintain it.[6]

Josh and Beth are examples of this. Josh runs his own business and Beth works for the NHS. During the Covid lockdown when the rule that six people could meet together indoors was made, they decided to meet together each week in their front room with two other couples. They would pray and worship passionately and encourage one another in faith. One day there was a knock at the door and a woman came in asking, 'Are you a church?' And they realized that they probably were. She came to faith in Jesus and over the next few months, and as the Covid restrictions lessened, the church that they had formed in their home grew. They welcomed new members, saw people come to faith using Discovery Bible Study (DBS) groups, gave generously to people in need around them and developed a simple life of discipleship together. Recently their new church community multiplied by planting two new house churches, led by the two couples who had been with them from the beginning. One of them said, 'We realized that if leading a church was simply doing what we had been doing together, we could lead a church like that.' Together with some DBS groups there are now over 60 people involved in this church two years after it started.

Myriad is developing a pathway to support small gospel-focused teams of two to six people led by a lay leader to plant a new church community. The training pathway provides a supportive community and resources to help them know how to lead the mission forward. It is flexible to adjust to the time people who are working are available as they lead these churches bi-vocationally. And it offers input that relates to the context they are in. Alongside this we are helping clergy to develop their role from delivering ministry to overseeing and supporting these teams. It is the 'both and' approach of new communities forming alongside established churches and we are hoping that through this initiative we can learn what new wineskins Jesus is forming for his Church and see church-planting movements released.

Many years ago the prophetic voice of Lesslie Newbigin challenged us to face the question about the pattern of our church life and how so much Christian activity is detached from Christians living their faith out in community together:

> I am suggesting that the only answer, the only hermeneutic of the gospel, is a congregation of men and women who believe it and live by it. I am, of course, not denying the importance of the many activities by which we seek to challenge public life with the gospel – evangelistic campaigns, distribution of Bibles and Christian literature, conferences, and even books such as this one. But I am saying that these are all secondary, and that they have power to accomplish their purpose only as they are rooted in and lead back to a believing community.[7]

Personal response: imagination

Read: Ephesians 3.20–21.

> Now to him who is able to do immeasurably more than all we ask or imagine, according to his power that is at work within us, to him be glory in the church and in Christ Jesus throughout all generations, for ever and ever! Amen.

This chapter has invited us to imagine different forms of church and the Church becoming a multiplying movement again. Where could you imagine a new church community forming in your community or network? Whom would it be with? Where would it be? What might your role be? Take that possible future church to God in prayer.

Thank God that this does not depend on you or your ability, but upon his power at work within you. Pray again for God's power to fill you and the church that you are part of.

Pray that through you and your church Jesus would be glorified.

6

A diverse leadership

Calling is not only a matter of being and doing what we are, but also of becoming what we are not yet but are called by God to be.

—Os Guinness[1]

John Lambie was the manager of the Scottish football team Partick Thistle. During a match one of his strikers Colin McGlashan was injured in a clash of heads with another player. The medic ran back to Lambie and said, 'Boss. He's totally concussed and he doesn't know who he is.' Lambie famously replied: 'Great. Tell him he's Pele and get him back on!'[2]

Who we think we are, how we perceive ourselves and how we understand our calling within the Church will significantly affect what we do. Our theology shapes our actions, our beliefs and our way of life, so thinking carefully about the nature of our identity and vocation as followers of Christ is vital. And when this comes to the leadership of a church community this is even more important. Who is allowed to lead and who has the power and authority to contribute their gifts and ministry is communicated in many ways. The structures of leadership, processes of discernment and appointments and the people who currently hold leadership positions are significant factors.

The early Church was an exciting place to be. In those early churches every Christian was a disciple gifted by the Holy Spirit, every disciple was a missionary and anyone could be a church planter, elder or apostle if that was what God had called them to be. This didn't mean that everyone had the same role or calling but there were no barriers between those roles. In chapter 6 of Acts Luke describes the seven deacons chosen to help distribute food to the widows and address a racial injustice. Their qualification was their spiritual life and character: wisdom and the Holy Spirit. They served food but we soon see them preaching and leading others to Christ. When Paul is guiding Titus in choosing the leaders of the churches in every town on the island of Crete, he uses similar criteria of godliness of character and faithfulness to the gospel. And finally, as he writes to Timothy overseeing the church in Ephesus, he outlines leadership roles of deacons, elders and overseers and details the faith in Christ and quality of character that they require. There was an openness to whom the Spirit was calling into different roles and to releasing people to fulfil what God was calling them to. People had different callings that complemented one another, serving the body of Christ in unity together.

As we read in the Gospel accounts and book of Acts there was great diversity among the 12 apostles and the cultures and backgrounds of those early believers. There were those regarded as outsiders and foreigners, collaborators and zealots. There were a good number of women, ranging from sex-workers to those with wealth and influence. We find diversity of age, gender, education, race, social class, heritage, temperament and theology described in different ways. The New Testament reveals that bringing such diversity together isn't always easy. But it is vital because this is how church works. God is glorified in each of us as we give a unique expression to his unique call on our lives, reflecting the unique pathway of our discipleship. But only when we come together in unity can his glory emanate from his Church. The more diverse our congregations are in terms of age, race, gender and experience, the more the glory of God is manifest as the spectrum of his grace is revealed.

The principle of the New Testament Church was unity and diversity. All serving one Lord, receiving one baptism and united in one body. Then there was a diversity of gifts, and a variety of leadership roles given to people such as apostle, prophet, teacher, pastor, evangelist, elder, deacon, overseer. Different people had different callings and functions and anyone with sufficient maturity could be called to these roles. There was a plurality and sharing of leadership throughout these different situations and the mission of the early Church was always conducted in teams. So it was organized but organic.

Again, we come to that Christendom cataract through a different lens and discover another aspect of its distortions: clericalism. Clericalism is the establishment of ordained ministry as a separate and higher class of Christian ministry which, by implication, diminishes the status and value of other ministries. It restricts certain aspects of the leadership and formation of church communities to ordained ministers. And it has distorted the pattern of the ministry of ordained leaders within the Church. Over the period of Christendom, the pattern of that ministry resulted in a male, highly educated and pastorally focused shape of ministry in the majority of denominations. As with Cessationism, no one signs up to these attitudes intentionally, but it has become a culture that has embedded itself in the Church which is often accepted without question. The elitism of these roles within the Church is shown in different traditions in different ways, from the megachurch pastor who is unaccountable, to the 'Father knows best' attitude of the Catholic tradition or the 'expert' preacher who is the only one able to teach the Bible in an evangelical church. Rather than simply being the particular calling of these people, the culture and structure of church that has formed around their roles has often disempowered the whole body of Christ.

Comparison with the biblical picture reveals some of the distortions of our current model. Not every disciple in our churches understands that God could call any one of them to step forward and lead within their church or context. Today there is often only one person who is in ordained leadership in a church and they seem to be the only one who can provide leadership, and many of the functions of ministry are reserved for them alone. Frequently there are no patterns of shared leadership and the role of most people in the church is to 'help' the minister, not to minister themselves. In some denominations, if you feel called to ordained ministry it is almost impossible to go on to be recognized as the leader of the congregation you belong to. Instead, after a national selection process, you have to leave your job, and that local congregation, to undergo years of training. The result is that often the people who are seen as qualified for this ordained ministry come from a narrow, educated and privileged group of people. And the consequence of this is that many people whom God might have called to these roles have been rejected or ignored, because of ageism if they are too old, sexism if they are a woman, racism if they are from a different cultural background, or intellectualism or elitism if they have not had the necessary education or social status. The seriousness of this is expressed by Pope Francis:

> Clericalism arises from an elitist and exclusivist vision of vocation, that interprets the ministry received as a power to be exercised rather than as a free and generous service to be given. This leads us to believe that we belong to a group that has all the answers and no longer needs to listen or learn anything, or that pretends to listen. Clericalism is a perversion and is the root of many evils in the Church.[3]

These injustices and distortions were never the intended outcomes. But we need the humility and courage to acknowledge that the Church in the UK has experienced serious decline and failed to connect with many people groups and communities, and I believe a significant reason for this is the leadership culture and structures in our churches. Around the world where the Church is flourishing the structures and patterns of leadership are flexible and not exclusive. David Garrison writes:

> In church planting movements, the laity are in the driving seat. Unpaid, unprofessional common men and women are leading the churches . . . Lay leadership is firmly grounded in the doctrine of the priesthood of the believer – the most egalitarian doctrine ever set forth.[4]

Katie (her English name) was a Chinese student at Leicester University. She came to faith at Holy Trinity, Leicester, through the student ministry there. God filled her with his Spirit and taught her how to pray and read Scripture and participate in mission and ministry. When she came to the end of her studies she returned to China. I remember the follow-up call I had with her a few months after she had returned. She explained that she was now leading a small church community. She described the pattern of their church life where they met together every day at 6.00 a.m. for prayers. They prayed intensely for the mission of God and worshipped, people spoke in tongues and prophesied. They were growing in number as people came to faith and she was currently raising up a couple of people in leadership. Her question to me was, 'Do you think what I am doing is OK? What would you do next?' My response was to weep with joy. And I reflected later that this could not have happened if she had still been in the UK.

The clergy–laity divide

At the heart of this issue are two words, 'clergy' and 'laity'. The word 'clergy' comes from the Greek word *klēros*, which means 'lot' or 'inheritance',[5] such as when Paul writes 'the promised Holy Spirit, who is a deposit guaranteeing our inheritance' (Eph. 1.13–14). It conveys a sense of blessing and status, but whenever it is used in Scripture it refers without exception to the whole people of God.

It never refers to a specially called elite subgroup of people. Laity comes from the Greek adjective *laikos*, meaning 'of the common people'.[6] *Laikos* is not in the New Testament, nor the Greek version of the Old Testament called the Septuagint. So we see our use of these terms is completely unbiblical and from the very beginning the use of them established the resulting distortion of clergy having a higher status than the rest of God's people. As Karl Barth said, 'The term "laity" is one of the worst in the vocabulary of religion and ought to be banished from conversation.'[7]

If we didn't recognize it from the words, we see it in the day-to-day practice. 'Real ministry' is carried out by 'clergy', those with special training and an extra endowment of spirituality. Laypeople exist to assist clergy in 'real ministry'. We say we believe in the priesthood of believers but look at our language and structures. Clergy do 'full-time' Christian ministry. We send people to Bible colleges to prepare for 'the ministry'. We install them in our congregations as 'the minister/pastor/priest'. Prayer is left to the clergy because they have special status before God. The sick have not been cared for until visited by clergy. Ask anyone for a definition of laity and it is nearly always given in terms of the negative: they do not administer the sacraments, they don't do full-time Christian ministry and they are just unpaid volunteers. We need a better vocabulary and theology. As Lesslie Newbigin writes, 'The missionary encounter with our culture for which I am pleading will require the energetic fostering of a declericalized, lay theology.'

And it is a system that harms clergy as well as laypeople. The clergy I know are consistently kind, generous, intelligent, faithful people who are serving God and his Church incredibly sacrificially. Yet within this system I see ordained leaders become isolated, overwhelmed, discouraged and burnt out as they try to manage the unreasonable expectations placed upon them. Often their denomination establishes institutional relationships with them which are transactional, often putting them under more pressure with insufficient support. Sadly, I see some of them fall into unhealthy coping strategies and others leave church leadership. Church leadership is hard work and ordained leaders are on the front line of the spiritual battle the Church is engaged in. Please pray for us.

And these cultures can create a codependent relationship between clergy and church members. Just as the people of Israel wanted a king despite being warned by God about what kings would demand from them, so congregations want an ordained minister who will deliver the ministry as they expect it without challenge or change, and in return they agree to support and finance them. Richard Lovelace warns of what happens in such a scenario:

> Pastors gradually settle down and lose interest in being change agents in the church. An unconscious conspiracy arises between their flesh and that of their congregations. It becomes tacitly understood that the laity will give pastors places of special honour in the exercise of their gifts, if the pastors will agree to leave their congregations' pre-Christian lifestyles undisturbed and do not call for the mobilization of lay gifts for the work of the kingdom.[8]

Gifted laypeople who lead companies, teach in schools, organize events or run charities often walk through the doors of a church knowing that their ministry in the world will not be empowered or equipped or recognized in that church community. And within the life of the church, they feel disempowered, unable to contribute their gifts and experience, and settle into this passive collusion that they are simply there to be a faithful worshipper.

The priesthood of all believers

It was never meant to be this way. The Bible teaches a completely opposite principle, the priesthood of all believers. Peter writes, 'But you are a chosen people, a royal priesthood, a holy nation, God's special possession, that you may declare the praises of him who called you out of darkness into his wonderful light' (1 Pet. 2.9).

Here Peter communicates what Paul implies in his image of the body of Christ, that it is the whole people of God who fulfil the priestly ministry of representing God to the world and bringing the world to God. It doesn't mean that there isn't particularity of roles for different people within the whole priesthood or body, but there is no divide between them. And it means that priestly ministry is not just the ministry which happens in church on a Sunday, but instead every single member of the body of Christ understands that they have been commissioned as a priest, a representative of Jesus Christ, in every aspect of their lives. The Church always exists in gathered and scattered forms, and every person is called to minister wherever Jesus sends them on mission.

The Church should reflect a shared and mutual ministry with each person expressing their differing callings and vocations. There should be no difference in the status of each member of the Church. Baptism is each Christian's ordination; we are all baptized equally into Christ, and we are all priests commissioned by Christ. Our callings and ministry arise from our shared discipleship. And this connects with one of the key areas God is wanting to restore in his Church: the authority and power Jesus has conferred on every one of his people by the presence of his Holy Spirit, not just a special few. Everyone gets to play. And this is what I mean by lowering the bar on who can lead. I am not reducing the significance of the responsibility we have when we lead God's people. I am saying that God can call anyone to lead a church and it is not dependent on qualification but on his call and the Spirit's empowering.

When I arrived as vicar of Holy Trinity Church, Leicester, I explained that one of my jobs as the leader of the church was to establish our missionary vocation as a church so that each person could discover his or her calling within that wider vocation. And so I would regularly ask church members, 'What is God calling you to do?' And I would receive the same reply: 'I've never been asked that question.' When Christians are simply expected to support the church's programme and fulfil slots on its rotas, no one asks you what your calling is. But when every disciple is seen as a minister and a missionary, and an agent of the kingdom of God, then asking that question is vital. Our understanding of calling is that God has made us with abilities and personalities and life experiences and spiritual gifts that all come together to enable us to fulfil a particular role or purpose in the work of his kingdom. So let me ask you that question. What is God calling you to do?

In order to give every member of the congregation the sense that they are a minister within the Church and that they share in the priesthood of all believers, one Sunday I ordained the whole of the evening congregation. I led them through the responses contained within the Ordinal for Priests and after they had declared their willingness to serve God in this way I then prayed the ordination prayer over them. Then they all put on cardboard dog collars. There were around 150 people there and it was an amazing sight. And then I explained that they weren't officially ordained because I am not a bishop and only bishops can ordain, but they were all ordained by God when they were baptized. This was their ordination as a minister and they should seek God's calling.

Where the Spirit of the Lord is there is freedom

At the time of writing, Operation World says that the Iranian church is the fastest-growing church in the world.[9] It is another example of how when the darkness reaches its darkest then the light shines more brightly, because the Christians there have to be willing to suffer for Jesus, and they are. But one of the most interesting aspects of this rapidly growing church is that its most significant leaders are women. In a country where women experience the greatest oppression and restrictions to their freedom, God in his grace has chosen women to lead his Church. Again, when you hear 'Church' you probably have to remove whatever picture you have from your mind. This is the underground Church. It is highly relational and without hierarchy. Outsiders who visit these churches often comment that they couldn't identify who the leader was as they met together and shared life. There are no church buildings or committees. Instead, new churches grow as new people come to faith and begin to meet secretly in small groups in homes and online. About 20 years ago, the number of Christian converts from a Muslim background in Iran was around 5,000 people. Today it is over 500,000.[10] It is a combination of the supernatural signs and wonders and the bravery of the saints who risk imprisonment or execution if they are caught sharing the gospel, a devotion to prayer, and a belief that every believer is a potential church leader and every church is a church-planting church. Ordinary Christians take responsibility for leading small churches in their homes, teaching Scripture and asking for the Holy Spirit's help to lead others to Christ. I think the significance of this is that in a church with no history or tradition of male leadership, under the leadership of the Holy Spirit, women are able to lead. A diversity of leadership has developed naturally as the Holy Spirit has inspired the growth.

Throughout Church history and around the world today, the Church that emerges from a move of the Holy Spirit has a diversity of leadership when compared with historic denominations established in Christendom. With regard to the ministry of women, women served at different levels of the Methodist movement. Many of the Class and Band leaders were women and some engaged in preaching and evangelism. Wesley noted that women were being fruitful in this way and he affirmed them and offered them training. Women such as Sarah Crosby, Mary Bosanquet and Grace

Murray were among the women leading as non-ordained ministers of the early Methodist movement. William Booth, pioneer of the Salvation Army, is often quoted as saying, 'Some of my best men are women.' George Fox who led the Quaker movement appointed a woman as his first minister. And David Yonggi Cho attributed the rapid growth of his church in Seoul, South Korea, the largest single congregation in the world, to the women who were leading most of the cell groups.[11] Jesus empowered women in his mission and the churches meeting in people's homes named many women as leaders of those communities. Without wanting to open up the whole debate about women in leadership, the culture and structures of church life in our nation have not released women into the fullness of their vocation and we have to take this seriously.

When it comes to cultural diversity, the Holy Spirit similarly breaks through the cultural barriers to leadership when he begins to move. In the Azusa Street Revival in 1906, anywhere up to 1,500 people would attempt to fit into the building. People from a wide diversity of backgrounds came together to worship: men, women, children, black, white, Hispanic, Asian, rich, poor, illiterate and educated. The intermingling of races and the group's encouragement of women in leadership were remarkable, as 1906 was the height of racial segregation, and 14 years prior to women receiving suffrage in the USA.[12]

And again, Wesley is our example as he taught non-ordained and non-seminary-trained men and women to be his lay assistants. He taught them to teach others, to evangelize and to preach. One critic of Wesley, Augustus Toplady, accused Wesley of 'prostituting the ministerial function to the lowest and most illiterate mechanics, persons of almost any class'.[13] We only have to look at the wonderful diversity of leaders who emerge when the Spirit breaks through structures and calls people to lead his kingdom work. From this we see our need to repent, to change our mind and believe for a new inclusive culture and new patterns of leadership in the Church.

And the reason this is so important is that if people from different cultural backgrounds are not represented in the leadership of their church, people from those backgrounds do not feel that they are welcomed or affirmed and it is much harder to enable them to bring their gifts to the life of the Church.

Apostolic and prophetic foundations

The other sign that it wasn't meant to be like this is what Paul teaches about leadership in Ephesians 4.11. He describes how the risen and ascended Jesus gave the apostles, prophets, evangelists, pastors and teachers to equip God's people for works of service. The significance of this is the picture of shared leadership it presents and a diversity of people leading. One of the common factors of the disciple-making movements and revivals taking place around the world and in Church history is that they are led by apostolic and prophetic leaders. Even as I write that sentence, I am aware of how difficult it might be to understand this language. We may not be familiar with all of the terms and so here is a summary of what I think the different types of leader mean within a church context.

Apostles: the Greek word for apostle, *apostolos*, literally means 'sent one', and the Latin word is *missio*, from which we develop the word 'mission'. An apostle was a role in ancient Greek and Roman cultures where a king would send someone as their ambassador to another country to protect and progress his interests.[14] We see this with Jesus' first apostles, who had a unique calling as he sent them to establish the Church at the beginning of its life. But the New Testament gives other people the title. For instance, Paul greets Andronicus and Junia and says they are outstanding among the apostles (Rom. 16.7), and Junia is a woman's name. So, the role of apostle continued in the Church beyond the 12 'capital A' apostles whom Jesus chose. Central to being an apostle is to lead the Church forward in mission. Apostles are the innovators, change agents and future thinking leaders of the Church. They like to be on the move and to step into new territory or activity.

Prophets: God-focused with a deep desire to enable people to come closer to Jesus and grow in their relationship with him, the prophets are the spiritual eyes and ears of the Church, as they have a sensitivity to the voice of the Spirit. They are often ready to challenge anything that undermines the Church's faithfulness to God, his word and his purposes. They equip the Church to hear God's voice and to be led in decision-making by the Holy Spirit. The early Church recognized many people in this role, such as Agabus, who prophesied a famine and Paul's arrest (Acts 11.28; 21.10–11).

Evangelists: the role of evangelists is to bring the good news to people who do not know Jesus yet. They have great confidence in the gospel and a desire to make Jesus known. Their gifting has a natural boldness and self-forgetfulness and all of this is given to the Church to inspire and equip people in their witness. They love to talk about Jesus and are often engaging storytellers. The capacity they have to bring people to a clear decision to put their faith in Jesus makes them the midwives of the Church.

Pastors: sometimes referred to as shepherds, pastors are vital in ensuring the church community is a place of love and deep relationships in which particularly the vulnerable members are cared for. They have big empathetic hearts and an emotional intelligence and sensitivity that enables them to understand the needs of the group and spot any potential threats or weaknesses. They ensure the Church is a place where healing and restoration are taking place. They often act as the 'glue' that holds the community together.

Teachers: the primary role of the teacher is to help the Church understand scriptural truth and grow in wisdom and faith in God. They help to cultivate a love of Scripture and ensure that there is good knowledge of the Bible and that it is used to guide decisions and engagement with the world. They are good communicators and explain biblical concepts in ways that make it easy for people to grasp.

The reason why these five roles are so significant is that they encapsulate the ministry of Jesus. Jesus was an apostle sent by God to this world and anointed by the Spirit to bring in God's kingdom. He was known as a prophet and clearly exercised prophetic ministry as he received supernatural communication from God. He was an evangelist seeking and saving the lost and he pastored the people he called to follow him, calling himself the good shepherd. And he was clearly a teacher as the Gospels are full of his teaching and people were amazed at the authority with which he taught. And the way that these roles enable the whole Church to look like Jesus is that they equip other people who have gifts and abilities in those areas to exercise them and together we grow to maturity in love.

But our current pattern and understanding of church leadership looks nothing like this. First, this is a team of leaders all working together, not one person. Leading a church as the only person in that leadership role was never Jesus' intention. Second, we have reduced the types of leader from five down to two. Whatever your church tradition, and whatever you call your church leader (priest, vicar, minister, pastor), I can almost guarantee that the role of teacher and pastor sums up what you are looking for from a leader. And we know this because if anyone describes their ministry as a pastor or a teacher we accept this and understand it, but if anyone says they are an apostle or prophet many of us don't know what to do with this. Christendom required only pastors/teachers because it was a static and maintaining culture in which the focus of church leadership was caring for the faithful. Cessationism taught that the roles of apostle and prophet ended with the end of the era of the first apostles and so no one was allowed to suggest that this was their calling.

Now that we are in a missionary situation, we need the apostles and prophets and evangelists. These leaders are like the sharp end of an arrowhead: they create movement and enable the Church to proclaim the gospel and bring the kingdom of God into new territory. God needs those who are gifted in this way to be leading his people. This doesn't mean we can't use the functional titles that exist such as minister or vicar, but we need to learn to discern and recruit people who will pioneer the mission of God. In fact, Paul actually says that apostles and prophets should be creating the culture of the Church: 'Consequently, you are no longer foreigners and strangers, but fellow citizens with God's people and also members of his household, built on the foundation of the apostles and prophets, with Christ Jesus himself as the chief cornerstone' (Eph. 2.19–20).

The foundation of a house determines its shape and height. The foundations of the Church are, first of all, Jesus and then apostles and prophets. When they lead together, the culture of the Church is one that listens to God and is led by the Spirit and is ready to act on what God says and to move in any way he calls us to. Churches will be places of innovation and creativity inspired by the Holy Spirit and with the capacity to develop new structures for growth. The ministry of the evangelists then flows out of this apostolic and prophetic culture. The evangelist is needed to enable new people to come to faith in these new places and their ministry is welcomed rather than resisted as it often is in our current maintenance-focused culture. As a Church we have to repent for rejecting these gifts and learn how to honour and receive them as they bring a different style and emphasis in their leadership.

And of course we still need teachers and pastors in this Church on the move. The teacher is needed to ensure that the innovation is guided by Scripture and in accordance with God's word and ways, and teachers will need to equip the new believers in faith. The pastor ensures that every new person is included in the Church, nurturing, healing and setting free all the new believers. This five-fold picture of leaders with different gifts in the Church can only happen with patterns of shared leadership. The current structures will need to flex and evolve to enable these different leadership gifts to be expressed. Paul says this isn't an optional extra; these are the leaders the risen Christ has given to his Church and so things will need to change.

It is vital that there is an evolution of roles and an experimentation of practice to help us discern what God is doing. Wesley believed that ordained ministers had a clear and important role in providing pastoral oversight of congregations and administering the sacraments, whereas the purpose of the Methodist preachers was preaching and evangelizing the lost. His was a 'both and' approach that reflected Jesus' teaching, but he called for a release from unnecessary restrictions. But in Wesley's day there was no permission given or acknowledgement of the possibility of different forms of ministry and the Church of England rejected the revival God was releasing through Wesley.[15] The challenge before us is to be open to how God wants our structures to evolve and release new people and new forms of leadership.

Here are three areas that will need our attention.

A culture of empowering leadership

When Paul taught about the five different kinds of leaders Jesus had given to the Church, he explained that their role was 'to equip his people for works of service' (Eph. 4.12). In this culture the people of God have a significant and shared involvement in the Church's ministry and the leaders equip them. This is a pattern of servant leadership in which leaders enable people to become and do more of all God is calling them to. In this culture, leaders share and give away ministry roles and create opportunities for people to take steps forward in ministry. Leaders will oversee and guide others' ministry and provide mentoring and accountability for them. There is nothing more joyful than to see someone grow into God's call.

Our Myriad team is developing training resources to help clergy learn to oversee and support laypeople to start new church communities. We believe this is the key that will unlock everything. We conducted some research with 20 laypeople who had planted new churches, called The Voice of the Lay Planter. They told us that the number one factor that enabled them to plant successfully was a champion. A champion is someone with organizational authority and ministry experience who walks alongside the lay leader to give permission for them to start to lead, guides them along the way, and encourages and champions them and what they are doing.

This is exactly what happened with Wole, who was a 22-year-old man from a Nigerian cultural heritage. Wole was coming to the end of an internship year at Holy Trinity Church, Leicester, during which he had been active in reaching out to young adults from different cultural backgrounds. As I prayed for him I sensed God was saying that he was calling Wole to plant a church. Wole confirmed his sense of this call. And without any formal training Wole led a team of 10 people to plant Imprint Church in the centre of Leicester. A church grew up of young adults from different cultures, many came to faith and came back to faith in Jesus. New people began to lead in Leicester and Wole led another team to plant a church in London. In Leicester, Holy Trinity provided practical support and mentorship in partnership with the Diocese of Leicester. It was an organized and organic experience in which new leaders were supported as they followed the call of God and hundreds of people have been included in church.

New leadership structures

If paid ministers begin to oversee more laypeople who are leading new ministries or small church communities or taking significant responsibility within the established church, there will be a need for new structures. The answer to the question of who can do what in church will change. As laypeople exercise the ministries traditionally exercised by clergy, really good and supportive relationships will need to develop and attention will need to be given to the importance of accountability and governance. This is not the clericalization of the laity, as some would say, because the new roles will be free of the rigid requirements of clergy and have flexibility. And the way that the different leaders and roles relate will evolve to enable them to share in leadership together and reflect different giftings.

New training pathways

Jesus' pattern, and that of the early Church, was to call people to be involved in mission and ministry and train them on the job as apprentices. This is very different from the formal discernment processes and academic course-based training found in historic denominations for ordained and authorized lay ministry. We need to enable people to respond to God's call and begin to lead once that has been discerned and not have to wait years until they have completed a training course and have a qualification. We need stages of development and recognition so that as people grow in leadership and their calling this can be recognized. And different people need different training and for laypeople who are leading they will need just-in-time training, accessed easily in the midst of their working and family life. We also have so much to learn about how leaders who have jobs and responsibilities outside of church leadership can lead in a healthy and sustainable way. In order to fulfil the missionary call of the Church we need all the people of God to bring all that they are to this work.

Herald the Weirdos

When Pete Greig was praying in a 24-7 prayer room he wrote a vision for this movement. It went viral and millions of people around the world have read it and been inspired by it. And that's because it is a vision of the Church as a movement. And so much of it resonates with what we have been talking about as he describes the people God is calling to follow him, to lead this movement and to live out the kingdom of God through their lives. As we finish thinking about the diversity of leaders the Church of tomorrow will need, let these words from Greig inspire you to believe that you can be a leader in the movement God is birthing:

Their DNA chooses JESUS. (He breathes out, they breathe in.) Their subconscious sings. They had a blood transfusion with Jesus. Don't you hear them coming? Herald the weirdos! Summon the losers and the freaks. Here come the frightened and forgotten with fire in their eyes. They walk tall and trees applaud, skyscrapers bow, mountains are dwarfed by these children of another dimension. Their prayers summon the hounds of heaven and invoke the ancient dream of Eden.[16]

Personal response: availability

Read: Ephesians 2.19–22.

Consequently, you are no longer foreigners and strangers, but fellow citizens with God's people and also members of his household, built on the foundation of the apostles and prophets, with Christ Jesus himself as the chief cornerstone. In him the whole building is joined together and rises to become a holy temple in the Lord. And in him you too are being built together to become a dwelling in which God lives by his Spirit.

Take some time to thank God for the church you are part of and for the leaders who serve in that church.

Reflect on this chapter, on where you see yourself within this family and temple. What is your calling and what is your contribution to God's temple?

Offer yourself to Jesus and ask him to call you afresh and anoint you afresh with the Holy Spirit.

Finish by saying or singing the words of the hymn 'Take My Life':

Take my life and let it be
consecrated, Lord, to thee.
Take my moments and my days;
let them flow in endless praise,
let them flow in endless praise.

Take my hands and let them move
at the impulse of thy love.
Take my feet and let them be
swift and beautiful for thee,
swift and beautiful for thee.

Take my voice and let me sing
always, only, for my King.
Take my lips and let them be
filled with messages from thee,
filled with messages from thee.

Take my silver and my gold;
not a mite would I withhold.
Take my intellect and use
every power as thou shalt choose,
every power as thou shalt choose.

Take my will and make it thine;
it shall be no longer mine.

Take my heart, it is thine own;
it shall be thy royal throne,
it shall be thy royal throne.

Take my love; my Lord, I pour
at thy feet its treasure store.
Take myself, and I will be
ever, only, all for thee,
ever, only, all for thee.[17]

7

A holy people

Holiness does not consist in doing extraordinary things. It consists in accepting, with a smile, what Jesus sends us. It consists in accepting and following the will of God.

—Mother Teresa[1]

In the second century, roughly 100 years after Jesus ascended to heaven, Diognetus was a wealthy man living in Greek society and was curious about the Christian faith. He had decided to ask one of the Christians he knew some questions and one day he received a letter in reply. It's more of a book than a letter as it contains 12 chapters and describes and defends the Christian life and faith. Within it is a description of the quality of life that the Christians are trying to live:

They exist in the flesh, but they do not live by the flesh. They pass their days on earth, but they are citizens of heaven. They obey the prescribed laws, all the while surpassing the laws by their lives. They love all men and are persecuted by all. They are unknown and condemned. They are put to death and restored to life. They are poor yet make many rich. They lack everything, yet they overflow in everything. They are dishonoured, and yet in their very dishonour they are glorified; they are spoken ill of and yet are justified; they are reviled but bless; they are insulted and repay the insult with honour; they do good, yet are punished as evildoers; when punished, they rejoice as if raised from the dead. They are assailed by the Jews as barbarians; they are persecuted by the Greeks; yet those who hate them are unable to give any reason for their hatred.[2]

Wow, what an amazing description of a creative Christian community. Completely engaged in the world and yet distinct from it. Marginalized and yet transforming the lives of people around them. And what is being described is holiness. Paul describes the Ephesians as:

God's holy people . . . For you were once darkness, but now you are light in the Lord. Live as children of light (for the fruit of the light consists in all goodness, righteousness and truth) and find out what pleases the Lord. Have nothing to do with the fruitless deeds of darkness. (Eph. 5.3, 8–11)

Paul's words resonate with those written to Diognetus; holiness is a movement from in to out, from the light of God's presence within us to us living in a distinct Jesus-shaped way in the world. The New Testament word that Paul uses for holy is *hagios*, which means set apart, separate and reserved for a specific purpose.[3] It follows that for Christians the call to be holy is a call to be set apart for God and his purposes alone. And that leads us to live distinctive lives in a world of different values and lifestyles.

Convex vs concave holiness

Back in the maths classroom again; you might remember the idea of convex or concave shapes. A convex shape curves outwards towards you and has a sense of fullness. And a concave shape curves inwards away from you and feels reductionist. Too much of our history in the Church has produced a concave holiness that has focused on sin avoidance and withdrawal from the world, banning different lifestyles such as dancing, drinking, going to the cinema.

It was legalistic and Pharisaical. Like the Pharisees who had 613 specific rules about behaviours that were banned, so the Christian faith became narrow and hollowed out. And the attitude that often accompanied this was a judgement and condemnation of the world around us.

It's not that we shouldn't repent of our sins. But we do this in order to be devoted to God alone and filled with the fullness of God. So being holy is not focused on a concave whittling away of things from our lives, but instead it is focused on being Christlike and offering a convex holiness that expands with the fullness of God towards the world. When Jesus comes to live in our hearts the holy one has come to dwell in us. This is the only reason we can hope to grow in holiness, because of the presence of the Holy Spirit. Without his presence, seeking holiness becomes a miserable dieting that avoids any possible contaminating experience. But with him it becomes the joyful journey of him setting us free from the things that spoil Christ's image in us. And we can confidently move towards the world around us, sharing our lives and carrying God's love and presence.

Jesus saves us from the kingdom of darkness and makes us holy and sends us into the world confident that he can keep us holy. Jesus is our example. The sinless perfect human being, who was completely set apart for God's purposes. His holiness was deeply attractive to 'sinners' and extremely challenging to religious people. The tax collectors, the sinners, prostitutes, people who felt rejected by the religious system all flocked to Jesus. Why does the Church's version of holiness so often seem the opposite of this?

Reportedly, Pope John Paul II captured it when he said:

We need twenty-first century saints with a spirituality embedded in our time. We need saints committed to the poor and necessary social change. We need saints who live in the world, who get holy in the world, and who are not afraid to live in the world. We need saints who drink Coke and eat hot dogs, who are netizens, who listen to iPods. We need saints who love the Eucharist and are not ashamed to drink a beer or eat pizza on the weekend with friends. We need saints who are in the world and who can taste the pure and good things of the world, but without being worldly. This is supposed to be us![4]

Taking God at his word

The reason that this is such a crucial issue for the Church of tomorrow is because holiness defines our relationship with the world. As we have outlined already, the post-Christian society around us often holds very different values from those of the Christian faith. Holiness requires us to live differently from those around us, not to be compromised in our behaviour but to remain engaged with the world.

Throughout this book we have been talking about Jesus' lordship, surrendering to him, obeying him out of love for him and learning to follow him in everything he taught. All of this implies that we know the will and word of Jesus. And we do. The Bible is the word of God. We don't have time here to argue for the authority of Scripture, but I want to offer one reason for allowing the Bible to be the authority of our lives: because it is what Jesus did. When we pick up the Old Testament it is the Bible that Jesus read. And as he began to deliver the most profound teaching that this world has ever known in the Sermon on the Mount, he stated that this was all about him fulfilling the word of God:

'Do not think that I have come to abolish the Law or the Prophets; I have not come to abolish them but to fulfil them. For truly I tell you, until heaven and earth disappear, not the smallest letter, not the least stroke of a pen, will by any means disappear from the Law until everything is accomplished. Therefore anyone who sets aside one of the least of these commands and teaches others accordingly will be called least in the kingdom of heaven, but whoever practises and teaches these commands will be called great in the kingdom of heaven.' (Matt. 5.17–19)

Jesus made it clear that Scripture is God's word and that his eternal purpose was to fulfil everything God had spoken. And he called us to put into practice the teaching of Scripture, and our place in God's kingdom is determined by our attitude to Scripture. When we step away from simple obedience as our default response to Scripture we distort our relationship with God's word; we come to it expecting to take what we want from it. We judge the Bible instead of allowing it to judge us. Holiness is about having the mind of Christ and we find this in Scripture. Paul talks about not being conformed to the pattern of the world but being transformed by the renewing of our minds. It is through Scripture we experience our minds being renewed through the conviction of sin, the call to Christlikeness and the understanding of what a holy life looks like.

In Ephesians Paul applies these principles to the lives of the church members there. He explains that in order for us to be filled with the Holy Spirit we must lead holy lives; the clue is in the title, Holy Spirit. If we are praying for the Spirit to fill us and revive us we must allow him to cleanse and shape us for his presence:

But among you there must not be even a hint of sexual immorality, or of any kind of impurity, or of greed, because these are improper for God's holy people. Nor should there be obscenity, foolish talk or coarse joking, which are out of place, but rather thanksgiving. For of this you can be sure: no immoral, impure or greedy person – such a person is an idolater – has any inheritance in the kingdom of Christ and of God. Let no one deceive you with empty words, for because of such things God's wrath comes on those who are disobedient. Therefore do not be partners with them. (Eph. 5.3–7)

Look at the subjects to which he applies God's word: to the Church, to your thinking, to your desires, to your communication, to your anger, to your work, to your relationships, to your sexuality. And he goes on to apply it to your marriage, and in chapter 6 to your parenting. Paul looks at every aspect of the life of a normal person and says that if you believe in Jesus, it will change how you handle this. The Letter to Diognetus shows that the lifestyle Jesus called all Christians to live had not changed 100 years later and it hasn't changed 2,000 years on.

Tim Keller writes:

The early church was strikingly different from the culture around it in this way – the pagan society was stingy with its money and promiscuous with its body. A pagan gave nobody their money and practically everybody their body. And the Christians came along and gave practically nobody their body and gave practically everybody their money.[5]

What that has looked like in past times of renewal is being courageous enough to open our lives to one another. We have referenced the accountability questions that were used in Wesley's Band meetings. Similarly, during the Welsh Revival Evan Roberts felt the Holy Spirit give him four requirements to be used as people gathered:

1 Confession of all known sin – if there is any unconfessed sin we cannot receive the Spirit.

2 Repentance and restitution – if there is anything doubtful in our lives it must be removed.

3 Obedience and surrender to the Holy Spirit – an entire giving up of ourselves to the Spirit is necessary.

4 Public confession of Christ – is a requirement of the Spirit.[6]

We may think this feels extreme but this is what raising the bar on discipleship looks like: asking our brothers and sisters to help us live a holy life devoted to Jesus. The surrounding culture and the devil who rules over it will seek to entrap and tempt us away from Christ. It is in community we find the strength to fight against this. The alternative is that we live a more comfortable but ineffective life and miss the joy of seeing Jesus fill us and use us for his glory.

A number of years ago, a Christian couple who were being persecuted in Iran had the opportunity to move to the USA, and they did. After living there for a period of time, the wife began to plead with her husband that they move back to Iran. 'Why?' he asked. She told him, 'It's like there's a satanic lullaby playing here, and the Christians are asleep. And I feel like I'm falling asleep! Please, let's go back!'

We may not have the option to move abroad, but we do have the chance to hear how Christ is calling his Church to wake up, to leave behind indifference and compromise, and to strengthen one another to live wholeheartedly for him.

Dirty holiness

The cost of sin is not just the way it undermines our relationship with God and others; it is that it undermines our ability to be led by the Spirit and minister his presence and power. One thing that changed from the old covenant to the new was the way holiness is transmitted. In the Old Testament holy things could become contaminated when they came into contact with unholy things (dead things, blood, disease, mould etc., see Leviticus). In the new covenant that Jesus instituted, unholy things became holy by touching him. When the woman with the issue of blood touched him, instead of Jesus becoming unholy and requiring purification, he released healing power that restored her. Jesus touched dead bodies and raised them to life, he touched those infected with leprosy and instead of him catching it they were healed.

We live by the high moral standards of the kingdom not because we are to be superior to and holier than others, but to be temples of the Holy Spirit carrying his presence and releasing his love and hope and healing. So, as we follow Jesus, we need to be willing to get our hands dirty. This is what it means to be a creative minority. Like Jesus we need to be in the places where those who are broken or imprisoned by evil or feel excluded can receive his light and love and hope from us; to build relationships, welcome and include everyone in God's love and allow the grace of Jesus to save and transform them. That means churches will be inclusive, messy places. No longer will they be places that expect people to behave before they belong. Instead, people start to follow Jesus and through coming into relationship with his people they are helped in their discipleship to work out how to obey Scripture.

A Jesus-centred Church

Frost and Hirsch use an analogy of fences and wells. If you are a farmer with a three-acre ranch, you can build a fence to keep your cattle in and other animals out. This would be a bounded set, where you work hard to define who is allowed to be in the Church and who is an outsider. But if you are a rancher with a huge amount of land you are not able to build fences around your whole property. So instead of building fences, you dig wells. So the animals keep returning to their water source.[7]

Too often in the past the Church has acted like a bounded set trying to determine who's in and who's out on the basis of belief or behaviour. The problem is that Jesus, the most holy person ever to live, didn't live like that. The creative church communities God is calling us to form are incarnational churches planted in the midst of people. This means that rather than drawing a border to determine who belongs and who doesn't, with a Jesus-centred community people are not seen as in or out, but as closer or further away from the centre, Jesus. Though some people are close to the centre and others far from it, everyone is welcome and anyone is potentially part of the community.

And at the same time it is a holy community with people being taught the truth and challenged to live it out in their lives. The purpose of discipleship is to make us holy and free from the bondages of sin, set apart and belonging to Jesus. It isn't to be a therapy session, in which our personal happiness is the goal. Jesus is radically inclusive as he welcomes us into relationship with him, but he loves us too much to leave us undisturbed in our sin and unchanged. He calls us to be holy. Holiness is Christlikeness.

A new creation

The second-century church father Irenaeus wrote that the Church is planted like the paradise of the Garden of Eden in the world. This is such a profound description of the Church. Within the beauty and goodness of creation Eden was formed as a place for the new human family to grow and thrive and to live with God and enjoy his shalom: literally his kingdom on earth. As Irenaeus reflected on this he realized that this connected with the redemptive purpose of the Church. Ever since Adam and Eve's disobedience and fall and their expulsion from Eden, God has been working to create again a new place where he can meet with his people. God plants new communities of his people in different places to bring into the world his redeeming and transforming presence through his people.

Paul in Ephesians talks about the new humanity God is creating in and through the Church, a community that he fills with his fullness in every way. The Church is to bring health and healing, reconciliation, justice and mercy in our relationships with one another and with creation and the world around us. This is the restorative community that the Church is called to be. It lifts our understanding of the Church from a human organization, with rotas and activities, and reveals the holy purpose and calling that every single church community owns. Note that the transformative healing work of God always comes through a community living like Jesus and offering him to the world.

When Bernice couldn't find an inclusive worship setting for her daughter to join, she and some friends started their own group. Bernice's daughter has Down's syndrome and as an adult the forms of adult church worship did not engage her and she didn't feel included. So they started WAVE – We're All Valued Equally – and when they gather for worship it is co-led by someone with and someone without disability. Bernice had no experience of leading a church when they started but with support from others she has found a way to form a new church community that expresses their call to include those who are excluded. Worship is creative and engaging and always involves food as the community gathers. The church has grown to over 40 people and one of the members said, 'I have to say, sadly and truthfully, that at almost every church my son has been treated like a terrible burden. Praise God, he led us to this small, diverse church where he was loved just like everyone else.'

One holy, catholic and apostolic Church

We find this statement in the Nicene Creed, written in the fourth century to counter the heresies of the day. This confessional statement allows people to affirm their commitment to the Church as has been revealed by Scripture. It addresses the issue of unity because there is only one Church across the world, the Church of Jesus Christ. It is defined as holy because it belongs to Christ, set apart for him. Catholic literally means worldwide rather than the denomination and apostolic demonstrates a commitment to Scripture as the teachings of the first apostles and the apostolic calling of the Church sent by Christ into the world.

The Nicene Creed remains a key confessional statement for the Church today. But what does that mean for our context? It might appear that the choice between a compromised mythology and a creative minority implies a divided Church. But this is not an option we are free to choose because Jesus prayed in Gethsemane, 'I pray also for those who will believe in me through their message, that all of them may be one, Father, just as you are in me and I am in you' (John 17.20–21). I believe God is calling his Church back to the Church from which the creed was birthed. The unity that creed expresses, and which Jesus prayed for, is a unity in him. It is one that makes Jesus Lord, and it is a unity that is surrounded by the unity of the Trinity, Father, Son and Holy Spirit, who surround us and are with us and within us.

Throughout the Church's history people have divided for many reasons. There will always be differences among us. And the New Testament allows for separation over issues of false teaching and sin. But the alternative that we have often opted for is an approach that covers up the differences with a thin veneer of apparent unity. Instead, the Church of tomorrow will have a holy fear of the Lord in which the identity of the Church as the body of Christ will cause us to do all we can to call people to a unity in Jesus, in which we refuse to separate over secondary issues but at the same time call people to follow Christ and obey his word.

Another way of expressing this is that the unity the Spirit is bringing to his Church will be seen as we find people who have heard the same sound, the same call, and are beginning to move together. This will be on the basis of a shared vision of the kingdom and the Church that is called to bring that kingdom on earth. And this will break down past divisions of denomination and tradition. Denominations defined themselves against other Christians over an aspect of practice or belief and terrible things were said and done that were justified because of the perceived superiority of that version of Christianity. I am excited that God is breaking down those divisions. Many people, especially those from Generations Y, Z and later, do not want to be labelled as Anglican, Baptist, Methodist etc.; instead, they belong to a certain congregation because of the relationships they have formed and a shared vision of the kingdom. New and exciting partnerships will form between churches because of this new freedom. This is how the unity that Jesus prayed for will be expressed.

Personal response: purity

Read: Ephesians 5.1–20.

Pray King David's prayer at the end of Psalm 139 (verses 23–24):

Search me, God, and know my heart;
test me and know my anxious thoughts.
See if there is any offensive way in me,
and lead me in the way everlasting.

Allow the Lord to show you the areas he wants to work on.

Find someone you could talk to about this and pray together.

Pray for the fullness of God to fill you so that there is an overflow of his Spirit to lead you into loving action in the world.

8

Prioritizing prayer

To clasp the hands in prayer is the beginning of an uprising
against the disorder of the world.

—Karl Barth[1]

The Yoido Full Gospel Church in Seoul, South Korea, is the largest
church in the world with over 800,000 members. When its then
pastor, David Yonggi Cho, was asked what the key reason was why
the Church in the West was so weak and yet the Church in Korea
was so vibrant, he simply said, 'You pray with your head, but we
pray with our heart.' And that heartfelt devotion leads millions of
Korean Christians to gather to pray every day all over their nation,
often as early as 5 a.m. in freezing temperatures.[2]

In our Christendom- and cessationist-shaped Church we have
often reduced prayer to a functional requirement of the Christian
life instead of our lifeblood and weapon in the spiritual battle. In
a benign world which contained little threat to the Church and
its teaching, and a version of the Christian faith that had little
expectation of the Spirit speaking and moving as we prayed, prayer
often became a simple affirmation of the truths of our faith as we
confessed our sins and asked for God's help. In the places around
the world that I have been privileged to visit where the Church is on
fire and growing, they pray differently. From an Orthodox church
in India, to an Anglican church in Mozambique, to a Pentecostal
church in Brazil there is a heartfelt desire, faith and power in their
praying that we rarely see in our UK church culture. The key is that
they prioritize prayer because they believe coming before God is
the most effective and powerful thing they can do. They surrender

their limited capacities and seek God's ability to act and move in this world. Instead of a short prayer asking for God's blessing on the plans discussed in a meeting, prayer is the plan and God is the source of everything they need.

The last revival to touch the shores of the British Isles began in 1949, with two old women in their eighties named Peggy and Christine Smith, who were greatly burdened because of the state of the body of Christ in their community. The Church in the little Hebridean island was in need of an awakening. These women took it upon themselves to pray. They spent hours in prayer, sometimes praying from 10 p.m. to 3 or 4 a.m. in their cottage. They sensed God encouraging them from Isaiah 44.3: 'For I will pour water upon him that is thirsty, and floods upon the dry ground: I will pour my spirit upon thy seed, and my blessing upon thine offspring' (kjv). And so they prayed this promise intensely.

During one of their prayer sessions, God impressed upon Peggy and Christine that he was calling a Scottish preacher called Duncan Campbell to visit them and that he would be used to bring about revival. They invited him and Duncan arrived for what was planned to be a two-week visit; he actually stayed about two years. In Duncan's first meeting, nothing major happened but one of the deacons encouraged him: 'Don't be discouraged, it is coming. I already hear the rumbling of heaven's chariot wheels. We will have another night of prayer and then we will see what God is going to do.' About 30 people gathered at a cottage that night to pray. At around three o'clock in the morning, God swept in and about a dozen were laid prostrate upon the floor. As they left the cottage that morning, they found men and women seeking God. No one seemed to think of sleep. Three men were found lying by the road-side in conviction, crying for God to have mercy upon them. The whole island was shaken.[3]

The ground of revival around the world and in history has always been prayer. Our prayer must always be, 'Lord, send revival and start with me.' Before he moves through us, he must move in us! It is the quality and quantity of the prayer that is significant. It is persistent even while there are no signs of anything happening. It is passionate and unrestrained as God shares his heart of love for the lost and his grief at the darkness that grips the land. Instead of polite prayer circles with an itinerary of prayer or formal litanies, prayer becomes urgent, tearful, with wrestling and groanings. If we long for a spiritual breakthrough in our nation we must rediscover this passion in prayer, we must rediscover the urgent cry of COME, LORD JESUS! COME, HOLY SPIRIT! If the Church in our nation doesn't rediscover the fullness of prayer, if we do not build altars on which we present ourselves and our prayers wholeheartedly to the Lord to consume with his fire, our nation will slip into a very dark future. We are not waiting for God. He is waiting for us. He is waiting for a people who will lay aside their dignity and schedules and cry out to heaven.

One of the questions I like to ask people is: 'If God were to answer your prayers for your community and your church, what would change?' Are our prayers focused only on the practicalities of our daily lives or do we pray for our church, our village or town or city, and our nation in a way that would see God's kingdom come? As an African bishop I know once asked, 'Do your prayers make God sweat?' Of course, nothing is impossible for God, but do our prayers match the awe and wonder of God and the size of the missionary task in our nation?

The spiritual realm

Ephesians contains three prayers of Paul and it is fascinating to compare Paul's prayer life with ours. In Ephesians 1.3–14, Paul opens his letter with an extended prayer of praise. The entire 12-verse passage is made up of one continuous sentence in the original Greek language. Paul gushes forth with declarations of God's blessings without stopping for a breath. He begins, 'Praise be to the God and Father of our Lord Jesus Christ, who has blessed us in the heavenly realms with every spiritual blessing in Christ' (verse 3).

This verse sets the tone for Paul's prayers: it is all about the grace, the salvation and the blessings that we have because we are included in Christ and which are now available to us from the heavenly realm. In his second prayer in 1.15–23 he prays for revelation and power, and these are the focus of the third prayer in 3.14–21 as he prays for God's fullness to fill his Church. What Paul's prayers reveal is that there is a spiritual realm that connects with our physical realm, and prayer is a way for us to engage in that connection. Prayer is the means through which the blessings of power and revelation are released to the Church in the physical realm.

And then he makes this extraordinary statement: 'And God raised us up with Christ and seated us with him in the heavenly realms in Christ Jesus' (Eph. 2.6). We are in the spiritual realm seated with Christ. Really, Paul? Paul is teaching the spiritual reality of everyone who believes in Jesus. He tells us that through God's saving power demonstrated in Christ's resurrection we already enjoy participation through the Holy Spirit in the heavenly realms where Christ resides. We are 'in Christ', we are eternally united with Christ; we are where he is. Our sitting and reigning with Christ is a position of authority, honour and triumph. We are inheritors and ministers of Christ's victory over Satan. This helps us to understand how despite our weakness and sinfulness we can go out into the world confident in the authority that we have in Christ. We are Christ's heralds, witnesses and priests and we are seated with him in the heavenly realm. And when we pray, we pray from this position of authority and we can bring the kingly reign of Jesus to bear in every situation we are in. Karl Barth, one of the greatest theologians of Church history, said, 'In Christian prayer we find ourselves at the very seat of government, at the very heart of the mystery and purpose of all occurrence.'[4] It can be expressed as sometimes praying to the throne, but sometimes praying from the throne declaring the truth of God and releasing his blessing and power.

The spiritual battle

This is vital to understand because Paul finishes his letter to the Ephesians by teaching them that they are involved in a spiritual battle with real spiritual forces: 'For our struggle is not against flesh and blood, but against the rulers, against the authorities, against the powers of this dark world and against the spiritual forces of evil in the heavenly realms' (6.12). It is only by understanding that we are in a spiritual battle that prioritizing prayer makes sense. There is an active enemy. There is a battle raging in the spiritual realm.

So, be honest with me. Does your local church ever talk about the spiritual battle we are in, does it equip you for this battle and does it do things that bring about spiritual victory and breakthrough? Even as I write that question, I am imagining a sense of confusion for some of us because it does not connect with our picture of the Church or our practices as local churches. The most important thing to understand is that our battle is not with people, 'with flesh and blood' (verse 6), but with the spiritual forces. We rightly shy away from militaristic comparisons and analogies because the language can make us feel we are conquering people and communities. Nothing could be further from the truth. The Christian mission is one of love, but love requires us to engage in confronting evil, not just through loving action, but with spiritual weapons. Jesus announced when he began his ministry:

The Spirit of the Lord is on me, because he has anointed me to proclaim good news to the poor. He has sent me to proclaim freedom for the prisoners and recovery of sight for the blind, to set the oppressed [or: captives] free, to proclaim the year of the Lord's favour. (Luke 4.18–19)

Twice in this ministry manifesto Jesus refers to people who have lost their freedom: prisoners and captives. I have always found the distinction between the two helpful. Prisoners can be released by an order of authority by which the prison guard is ordered to unlock the prison door. On the other hand, captives who have been illegally made hostages are set free when an SAS team bursts in and breaks down the door and subdues the enemy. Jesus says that he has come to do both. As we continue Jesus' mission in the world this is something of what I think God is wanting to do now in and through his Church. It will be a ministry Jesus is doing within the Church as he sets us free, but that work is so that we can be his people bringing others into the glorious freedom of God's children.

The Christians living in Ephesus were up against it. The spiritual climate was hostile with temples to Artemis and Diana. The ethics and morals of that society opposed God's ways. And Paul helps them to understand that what is happening around them is because of the spiritual forces of darkness which are at work over them and around them. We now live in a similarly spiritually hostile culture. Very real powers seek to stand in the way of God's kingdom being established on earth. Some parts of the Western Church have constructed a picture of reality that denies the existence of a real personal enemy with the title Satan or the devil. Although it can seem strange to name him and talk of demons and the devil, for the rest of the worldwide Church it is actually strange to have a version of the Christian faith without this understanding. C. S. Lewis in his brilliant book on the spiritual battle, *The Screwtape Letters*, said that, 'There are two equal and opposite errors into which our race can fall about the devils. One is to disbelieve in their existence. The other is to believe, and to feel an excessive and unhealthy interest in them.'[5] I am convinced one of the steps God is inviting us to take into the future is to learn how to win spiritual battles with the armour Christ has won for us.

Saint Patrick knew what it was to be in a battle. God had sent him to proclaim the gospel in Ireland. In AD 405 when he was 16, Irish raiders had taken him captive from his home in Roman Britain and used him as a slave working as a shepherd in Ireland. In these harsh conditions God broke into Patrick's life and Patrick grew in devotion to Christ. He learned to pray as he worked, and wrote about how the cold did not bother him as he rose before the dawn or stayed out all night on the mountains to pray. He managed to escape and back in Britain he had a vision of the Irish people crying out: 'We beg you come walk with us again!' He said yes to God's call and was ordained as a bishop by the church and sent as a missionary to Ireland.[6]

This was no easy mission-field; in fact, the Roman Church saw the Irish as barbarians who could not be reached with the gospel. There were a bewildering number of gods, goddesses and beliefs in ancestral and other spirits. Patrick faced enormous opposition from the Druids, the powerful priestly caste of that society. On one occasion when Patrick was preaching, a powerful magician interrupted him and blasphemed the name of Jesus. Immediately a lightning bolt struck the magician and he died.

Patrick himself lived with constant awareness that he might be killed for his faith. He wrote of being tormented by demonic spirits as he fasted and prayed. But he prayed continually and followed the leading of the Holy Spirit. Apparently, the gift of the Spirit that Patrick and his missionaries treasured most was the gift of discernment of spirits as they tried to work out what was happening in the spiritual realm and battle around them.

The fruit of Patrick's ministry was incredible. He preached the gospel and healed the sick and raised the dead, and thousands of people came to faith. He formed monasteries that trained and sent out teams to plant hundreds of local churches. Society was transformed as he ended the slave trade in that nation and the bloody feuds between the different tribes reduced as many of their kings came to faith. Despite the success of his mission, Patrick received significant opposition from other bishops in Britain because he had not completed sufficient theological education and his knowledge of Latin was poor. But it was Patrick's devotion to Christ and courage to set the people of Ireland free from their spiritual bondage that mattered. Here is his own reflection on his ministry:

> However ignorant I was, in the last days [I] dared to undertake such a holy and wonderful work – thus imitating somehow those who, as the Lord once foretold, would preach His Gospel for a testimony to all nations before the end of the world. So we have seen it, and so it has been fulfilled: indeed, we are witnesses that the Gospel has been preached unto those parts beyond which there lives nobody.[7]

Gearing up

Statistically, more civilians die as a result of the devastating effects of war than actual combatants. This is because they are living in a war zone without being trained and without protective armour or weapons. This is now the danger facing the followers of Jesus today. We are going about our daily lives as if life were a playground instead of a battlefield. Paul refuses to leave the Ephesian Christians as needless casualties of war and so he teaches them how to stand and fight: 'Put on the full armour of God, so that you can take your stand against the devil's schemes' (6.11).

The armour is the salvation, righteousness, faith and truth that Jesus has won for us, with the feet of a herald longing to take the gospel into new places and a sword of God's word with which to engage the enemy. It is in prayer that we appropriate these gifts for ourselves and it is in prayer that we win the spiritual battle with them. And the picture that Paul paints is of the Church standing firm in the midst of the battle and advancing as it has opportunity, because there is only front-facing armour. There is no retreat envisaged in this picture. At this time I believe God is raising an army to fulfil his kingdom purposes. All that Paul has been writing about and we have been engaging with is to equip an army. Just as in the vision of revival in Ezekiel 37 where the dry bones rise with breath in them to become an army, so God is calling his people to rise up and fight to see his kingdom come.

J. C. Ryle summarizes:

Necessity is laid upon us. We must fight. There are no promises in the Lord Jesus Christ's epistles to the seven churches, except to those who 'overcome'. Where there is grace, there will be conflict. The believer is a soldier. There is no holiness without a warfare. Saved souls will always be found to have fought a fight.[8]

In the Falklands War in 1982 the British navy commandeered cruise ships and turned them into battleships. What that refit involved was throwing out the entertainment furniture and installing weapons in its place. This happened to SS *Canberra*. They cut off large parts of it and built three helicopter decks in three days, and put 3,000 troops on board instead of the usual 1,700 holidaymakers.[9] The Church is meant to be the battleship where we get trained and equipped, not a cruise liner. And in the rummage sale where we throw out understanding and practices that have built up in our Christendom cessationist Church, this will create space for the spiritual weapons Christ has won for us and which we need.

Five key practices

Paul finishes his letter by writing, 'And pray in the Spirit on all occasions with all kinds of prayers and requests. With this in mind, be alert and always keep on praying for all the Lord's people' (6.18). So there are all kinds of prayers. I think that the prayers we are praying and the life of prayer in our churches are good and acceptable. It's just that this pattern of prayer was shaped by a different context and it stops short of what is needed for tomorrow. So here are five spiritual practices that enable God's people to take steps forward into those different kinds of prayer. And these help us to stand and see the victory of God prevail in our lives. These are far from a comprehensive description of the prayer life of a disciple of Jesus Christ, but they are areas that connect with Paul's teaching about the spiritual battle and are often weak in the current pattern of Christian life in our Church today.

Waiting on God

Waiting for the Lord is not a passive activity, but is an active desire to depend on God. It means that we are not moving from any place or situation until God leads us. It is a spiritual waiting and is the equivalent of what Paul teaches in Ephesians 6.14, to 'stand firm'. In uncertain times we are able to wait as individuals and churches for God to speak and to show himself and what he is calling us to do. I believe going slower will often be a mark of the Church of tomorrow. Instead of feeling the pressure to always be busy or anxious to come up with our own solutions, we choose to wait on God. And waiting is possible because Jesus is Lord and we can trust in his sovereign reign. There is rest in the victory Jesus has won for us. We wait quietly and patiently, seeking strength in the Holy Spirit, but we also wait expectantly for God who is working for our good, constantly coming before God in prayer and waiting for him to speak. God is working in the waiting and, more significantly, we are changed as we wait on him. Practices of silence and journalling can help us in these times. Through this process God is teaching us and leading us to the place where we are ready for what he is going to do. As Andrew Root writes: 'To wait is to be catechized, to enter a school that forms us to see the action of a living God . . . Prayer itself is waiting.'[10]

Praise and worship

Sung worship is a powerful weapon. From the Old Testament Levites and trumpeters leading Israel into battle, to Paul and Silas praising God in jail, or to the songs that the Holy Spirit inspired in every past revival, God has made it clear that praise is more than an offering of worship to him; it is a weapon in the spiritual battle. Praise is an act of devotion to God and resists the forces of evil. Worship changes the spiritual atmosphere around us; as we lift up the name of Jesus the darkness has to retreat. As the missionary Amy Carmichael reportedly said: 'I believe truly that Satan cannot endure it and so slips out of the room – more or less – when there is a true song.'

The one instruction that Paul gave in Ephesians about worship was to speak 'to one another with psalms, hymns, and songs from the Spirit. Sing and make music from your heart to the Lord, always giving thanks to God the Father for everything, in the name of our Lord Jesus Christ' (Eph. 5.19–20). Passionate sung worship marks the Church around the world and in revival history, yet in our churches today singing is often little more than a break in the liturgy. And our experience of small groups in our churches often does not include sung praise and worship due to embarrassment! In the creative church communities God is calling us to form, coming into God's presence in sung worship, declaring his praises and strengthening ourselves in him will mark our gatherings.

Contending prayer

Contending prayer is needed either when there is a battle over something and the enemy is seeking to kill, steal or destroy something (John 10.10) or when there is a battle against something God has called us to do. This type of prayer moves beyond simply interceding and bringing our needs to God, to one in which we take our authority in the spiritual realm and bind and loose and declare all that God has spoken to us and promised. It is based on a clear conviction of what God has said or is calling us to do, and from this we can stand in his authority and we pray and pray until we see that battle won. To contend is to fight or reach for something. Paul gives an example of this when he writes to the Colossian Christians: 'Epaphras, who is one of you and a servant of Christ Jesus, sends greetings. He is always wrestling in prayer for you' (Col. 4.12).

As I interview people who are planting churches all over England, the common theme is that they credit the success of being able to plant a church to persistent prayer. The Redeemed Christian Church of God (RCCG) is an example of this. The RCCG is a Nigeria-based denomination with churches all over the world. In 2000, from its church Jesus House in London, it started establishing churches all over the country and now has over 800 parishes, as it calls them. When it sends a small team of people to start a new church in a new area it supports this team in a number of ways and one of these is through prayer. Before the practical work of planting a church begins, a prayer team goes into the area and prays persistently for a number of weeks. They will walk the streets and pray over the area. They listen to God and specifically pray against the spiritual powers that they identify working in the area, and they dedicate that area to Jesus and declare his lordship over it.

Fasting

Jesus begins his ministry with 40 days of spiritual warfare as he fasts and wrestles with the enemy. And when he starts to teach about spiritual practices in the Sermon on the Mount, he assumes that everyone understands the need to fast. He says, 'When you fast . . .' (Matt. 6.16). He gives this teaching alongside his teaching about prayer and financial giving, fasting is seen as one of the basic spiritual disciplines of the Christian life. Again, our sisters and brothers around the world know this and when I visited a church in India they explained that every member of the church fasts and prays each Friday. Then at the end of the day they gather together for a meal and to pray together and share testimonies. My practice is to have a regular pattern of fasting, often having a weekly day of prayer and fasting, and then use it more intensively around issues or times where I sense the spiritual battle, where I will fast for a longer period of time.

The biblical principle of fasting is a process of giving up something, primarily food, in order that we might devote our heart, mind, soul and strength to God in a more intense and focused way. It gives a physical expression to our desire for God and to be utterly dependent upon him. Although fasting is often something we do personally as part of our life of prayer, the Bible also refers to a number of corporate fasts when the people of Israel were in a desperate situation and needing a spiritual breakthrough. The testimony of the Church across its history is that fasting is a powerful way to engage in spiritual warfare. Significant shifts and major breakthroughs can come as a result of fasting and prayer.

Blessing

I love the Local Houses of Prayer movement across the UK where local Christians meet together to pray for their neighbourhood. A focus of that prayer is to pray the blessing of God in that place and release his presence there, to pray for the kingdom to come. Their testimony again and again is that they pray the blessing of God for months until something seems to shift. When we understand that we are priests and citizens of heaven, seated with Christ, and we have his authority to bless the workplace, school, shops and neighbourhoods that God has placed us in, then we pray from the throne room where we are seated, releasing God's peace and love into the lives of people around us.

Personal response: standing firm

Read: Ephesians 6.13.

> Therefore put on the full armour of God, so that when the day of evil comes, you may be able to stand your ground, and after you have done everything, to stand.

Read the whole of the passage about the spiritual battle from Ephesians 6.10–17.

For each piece take some time to thank God for that aspect of his spiritual protection and provision. Make the statement 'I put on the . . .' and then pray for God's help to live in a way that is consistent with that piece of armour.

Think about which of the five practices of prayer you feel you need to grow in and make a plan to begin to engage in that type of prayer.

As we have heard the story of Patrick, here are some of the verses from his wonderful prayer often called 'Patrick's Breastplate':

> I arise today
> Through a mighty strength, the invocation of the Trinity,
> Through belief in the Threeness,
> Through confession of the Oneness
> of the Creator of creation.
>
> I arise today
> Through the strength of Christ's birth with His baptism,
> Through the strength of His crucifixion with His burial,
> Through the strength of His resurrection with His ascension,
> Through the strength of His descent for the judgement of
>   doom.

I arise today, through
God's strength to pilot me, God's might to uphold me,
God's wisdom to guide me, God's eye to look before me,
God's ear to hear me, God's word to speak for me,
God's hand to guard me, God's shield to protect me,
God's host to save me
From snares of devils,
From temptation of vices,
From everyone who shall wish me ill,
afar and near.

I summon today
All these powers between me and those evils,
Against every cruel and merciless power
that may oppose my body and soul.
Christ with me,
Christ before me, Christ behind me,
Christ in me, Christ beneath me,
Christ above me,
Christ on my right, Christ on my left,
Christ when I lie down, Christ when I sit down,
Christ when I arise,
Christ in the heart of every man who thinks of me,
Christ in the mouth of everyone who speaks of me,
Christ in every eye that sees me,
Christ in every ear that hears me.[11]

Conclusion

Beware of harkening back to what you once were, when God wants you to be something that you have never been.

—Oswald Chambers[1]

What I saw was the British Isles, as in a bird's-eye view. A kind of haze was over the whole, like a green fog. And then little pinpricks of light began to appear from the top of Scotland to Land's End. Then the Lord seemed to draw me closer to these lights, and I saw that they were fires that were burning. They were multiplying from the top of Scotland to Land's End. Then I saw lightning come and strike those fires, the brightest spots particularly, and there was a kind of explosion, and rivers of fire flowed down. Again, the sense of direction was from the top of Scotland to Land's End. But some of those rivers of fire didn't stop there. They went right across the Channel and didn't stop there. They went right across the Channel and spread out into the Continent.[2]

This was a prophetic vision given to Jean Darnell. Darnell was an American pastor and prophet who launched Foursquare Church in the UK and founded a Bible college. As she prayed about this vision she came to understand that those fires were groups of people whom God would make intensely hungry for New Testament Christianity. They would start asking: Where are these people so full of the power of the Holy Spirit? Where are these miracles? Where is this growth, this vitality, this courage, this boldness that these people had? Is that for today; can we have it today? Should the Church be this way?

The vision was given in 1967 and this helps us to understand the broad timescale of God's reforming work. I believe this is the era we are living in today and the vision describes the Church of tomorrow we have been picturing. The creative communities are the fires springing up all over the country, making Jesus Lord, filled with the Spirit, living as missional disciples seeking to see God's kingdom come in their communities. And although we have talked about the Church of tomorrow, we don't have to wait for tomorrow; we can step into this today. Jesus said, 'Don't you have a saying, "It's still four months until harvest"? I tell you, open your eyes and look at the fields! They are ripe for harvest' (John 4.35). God is preparing his Church for the harvest of people he is calling into his kingdom. Tomorrow begins today.

This book has been an invitation to hold the plumb line of Scripture, the Church in revival in history and the rapidly growing Church around the world up against the Church that you and I belong to in the West and to note the differences. This takes humility and courage but it is also life-giving because these stories of the Church contain the life we are being called to live. The new thing God does is always a new old thing because it is sourced in his eternal nature. And so the Lord is saying again to his Church: 'Stand at the crossroads and look; ask for the ancient paths, ask where the good way is, and walk in it, and you will find rest for your souls' (Jer. 6.16).

God knows how to rescue his people and to renew and revive them. There is no pressure to rush into activity. All that God will do will come from the rest we enjoy in Jesus Christ and his presence in us. We can be the non-anxious presence our communities need. The defining mark of those ancient paths will be that we are following Jesus, that we are centred on him and being shaped by him in all we do. We will not be defined by a denomination or tradition. Instead he is calling together a remnant people who recognize in one another a desire for the kingdom and the renewal of the Church and revival of the nation.

The wedding of the bride

In Ephesians Paul describes this work of preparation as a bride being prepared for her wedding day:

> Christ loved the church and gave himself up for her to make her holy, cleansing her by the washing with water through the word, and to present her to himself as a radiant church, without stain or wrinkle or any other blemish, but holy and blameless. (Eph. 5.25–27)

The Church is the bride of Christ. It does not belong to us, we belong to Jesus. We are made righteous through his blood and he clothes us in his righteousness and he is making us holy. And the image of the bride of Christ is a vision of our eternal destination. The Church of tomorrow is ultimately the Church united with Christ in his eternal kingdom. The apostle John received this revelation of the eternal Church that the book of Revelation records:

> I saw the Holy City, the new Jerusalem, coming down out of heaven from God, prepared as a bride beautifully dressed for her husband. And I heard a loud voice from the throne saying, 'Look! God's dwelling place is now among the people, and he will dwell with them. They will be his people, and God himself will be with them and be their God. "He will wipe every tear from their eyes. There will be no more death" or mourning or crying or pain, for the old order of things has passed away.' He who was seated on the throne said, 'I am making everything new!' (Rev. 21.2–5)

This is ultimately the Church of tomorrow, a bride coming to meet her bridegroom. What a joyful moment that is; I will never forget the moment when my wife Bridget stood in front of me and we made our vows to one another. I have taken many weddings and I have never seen a groom who is not blown away by the sight of his bride walking towards him. This is the moment of *palingenesia*, when everything is renewed. And as the whole of creation is made new the Church is centre stage; the relationship God had intended with his people is completely restored. This is the culmination of the whole of salvation history as Christ returns and is united with his Church, when we will know Jesus face to face, and the whole of creation is lit up by his presence.

Having this eternal picture in our hearts and minds will strengthen us and sharpen us for the journey ahead. It brings a strength and an urgency to our lives. This is what awaits us and we are willing to suffer today for the eternal reward we will receive. This is the spiritual truth of who we are in Christ and we are determined to live a life worthy of this. And we long for many people to be saved and enter into this eternity with us. Richard Baxter was a Puritan pastor in the seventeenth century, whom God used significantly to evangelize the town of Kidderminster. He suffered chronically from many serious illnesses and early in his life he was facing death. In his book *The Saints' Everlasting Rest* he tells us the source of his endurance and motivation. As Baxter faced death he began to meditate on heaven, the glory of Jesus Christ that awaited him. Miraculously he was saved from death but for the rest of his life he was committed to meditating upon heaven for at least half an hour every day. It was carrying a vision of Jesus and our eternal life with him that sustained him in his ministry despite all the challenges he faced.[3]

Find your running mates

On 12 October 2019, Eliud Kipchoge became the first human being to run the 26.2 miles of a marathon in under two hours. It was an incredible feat as he finished the course in 1 hour 59 minutes and 40 seconds. Apart from being a wonderful athlete who had won numerous world marathon titles, it was the team of runners who ran with him that helped him break what had seemed an impossible barrier. Kipchoge had 41 elite long-distance runners running with him in teams of seven, setting the pace and reducing wind resistance. This is the reason that this isn't an official world record: it wasn't an individual effort, it was a team effort. But it was also the only way he could have done it.

Jesus never sent his disciples out alone. They always went in teams of at least two, even when he sent them to fetch a donkey or find a room. You need to be part of a team, a creative community, to see how to run this race together. Not everyone in the Church will choose to follow Jesus into the future he has for his Church, and this future will not happen with everyone moving together at the same pace. The Anglican theologian and pastor Martin Thornton labelled this approach 'multitudinism', an approach that attempts to move the multitude simultaneously, and that is naively unaware of the way God operates and renews his people by starting with a few, the remnant, who catch the fire and then enable others to join in.[4] So you will need a community of those who share this vision of the Church and are willing to follow Jesus into the future.

The reason that understanding this is important is because you will face resistance and opposition. Every past reformation and revival that we celebrate today as the work of God was rejected by significant numbers of the Church in its day. So we are back to the creative minority, the small amount of leaven in the dough, small communities that God will use to change the whole Church. We find others who are willing to join the dance of God's Spirit where we stir one another to pray prayers of faith, obey God's word, give our time and hearts and souls to the work of seeing God's kingdom come into the lives of those around us. Arthur Wallis writes, 'We must be miniature forerunners, each in our own sphere. It is not enough to prepare the way in our own hearts; we must prepare the way in the hearts of others.'[5]

This is all that the first disciples did. They were gripped by a vision of Jesus (Acts 1), filled with the Spirit (Acts 2), proclaiming the gospel and healing the sick (Acts 3), refusing to be intimidated by opposition and praying (Acts 4), feeding the poor (Acts 6). From this creative community in Jerusalem God scattered the believers, and the gospel reached the ends of the earth. God can do this again in our nation and he will do it through small communities of people seeking to live like that early Church.

Perhaps you are a leader of a church with a strongly estab-lished tradition of Sunday worship. Why not start something new alongside and not even on a Sunday, gathering together a group of people? Make a conscious shift away from spending all of your time maintaining existing structures and towards growing people who are disciple-making disciples of Christ. Or you might be part of a church with no small groups meeting to grow in faith and follow Jesus together. Why not start one? Perhaps there is no clear way to express what God has stirred in your heart as you read this book. Find one or two others who share your vision of God and his Church and begin to pray. If God is speaking to you he will be speaking to others; he never leaves us on our own.

Guard your heart

The proverb warns us, 'guard your heart, for everything you do flows from it' (Prov. 4.23). The key to navigating the territory we are entering into and being the Church we have been describing will be having a heart that is open to new possibilities. And in times of challenge and change we need to pay attention to our hearts so that they don't become hardened by all that this involves. So as we finish, here are three elements to keeping our hearts soft and open to what Jesus is calling us to.

1 A posture of humility

The archbishops have presented the Church of England with three guiding words about the Church of the future: simpler, humbler and bolder. I believe these to be inspired by the Holy Spirit to guide the Church. A posture of humility allows us to acknowledge that we haven't got everything right, rather than trying to defend ourselves. This acknowledgement liberates us to hear Jesus' invitation to follow him and discover who he is calling us to be. And we have to be willing to be those disciples who learn and grow in ways we didn't expect to or even want to before. Eric Hoffer explains that in a time of drastic change it is the learners who inherit the future. Our humility must foster a willingness to live with ambiguity and things we don't know. We acknowledge our lack of competence and choose to be an amateur in the new rather than an expert in the old. Instead of seeking great successes or to build impressive programmes, we simply take small steps of obedience. It was William Faulkner who encouraged us to make footprints and not monuments, because a monument marks the place in history where we once were, but a footprint is part of the ongoing movement.[6] Let's keep making footprints, trying to place our feet wherever Jesus is leading us.

2 Life-giving relationships

Having courage to find those God is calling us to run with and form new relationships with, and to find communities beyond the current structures will be vital. Being with those who give you life will sustain you in this journey. And finding the people with new gifts and experiences, from different backgrounds, forming rich intercultural communities will be a sign that the Spirit is leading us. Such relationships become the place where God can bring his word and inspire us and sharpen us through one another. These relationships 'hold us' and keep us going when we are tempted to give up, and they are places where we discern and process things amid the confusion and unknown nature of the journey. And they are relationships where we are released into more of what God is calling us to. Leadership will not be primarily based on positional authority or hierarchy, but rather on relationship and calling with people, inviting others into leadership and walking together.

3 Experimentation and entrepreneurship

Because we are heading into unknown territory the culture of the Church will increasingly be entrepreneurial. Church cultures will value experimentation and the majority of church leaders will be leading small communities of faith bi-vocationally. This will bring the lessons and gifts of the wider community into the Church. Attitudes of curiosity, imagination, risk-taking and playfulness will allow us to explore the new territory Jesus is leading us into. Music and the arts will be at the heart of this move of God. Partnerships between churches, businesses and charities will form in local communities. Churches will launch businesses in order to fund life and mission. Entrepreneurial church planters will engage and gather communities of faith in the marketplace.

Following the wild goose

If you visit the island of Iona, off the west coast of Scotland – where Columba founded his monastery in the sixth century – you will find paintings and sculptures of a fascinating image: the wild goose. The Celtic Christians had a name for the Holy Spirit that has always challenged me, *gèadh-glas*, which translates as 'the wild goose'. The experience of Columba and his community following the Holy Spirit on mission in that pagan culture was that it was like following a wild goose. The name hints at the unpredictable, untameable, wild and always on-the-move nature of the Holy Spirit. Jesus said that this would characterise those who live by the Spirit: 'The wind blows wherever it pleases. You hear its sound, but you cannot tell where it comes from or where it is going. So it is with everyone born of the Spirit' (John 3:8).

It was the 'wild goose' nature of the Holy Spirit that called Patrick back to Ireland and carried Columba to Iona. God used both men to make a huge impact on the Britain of their day. As we sense God's call to his Church in our nation at this time, the life he is calling us to will mean following the wild goose. It will involve leaving behind well-worn paths and heading into unchartered territory. But as long as we keep in step with the Spirit day by day, God will get us to where he wants us to be.

As we finish, I offer you this prayer. I dare you to pray it!

Holy Spirit,
Wild goose of the Almighty,
Disturb me where I have settled
   and release me to fly with you.
Set me on fire with love for you
   and give me courage to obey your voice.
In the dark places, let me carry your light.
With the broken, fill me with compassion
   and minister your healing.
Send me to the lost, that they may find life in you.
In humility I offer myself afresh to you so that, with others,
   you may form and forge us to be a people for yourself,
   living for your glory.
Amen

Notes

Introduction

1. Thomas Merton, *He Is Risen* (Allen, TX: Tabor Publishing, 1967), p. 1.
2. Phyllis Tickle, *The Great Emergence: How Christianity is changing and why* (Grand Rapids, MI: Baker Books, 2012), p. 10.
3. Bob Mumford, *Stepping Over the Threshold* (Cookeville, TN: Lifechangers Publishers, 2020), p. 2.
4. Linda Woodhead, 'Time to Get Serious', *Church Times*, 31 January 2014: <https://www.churchtimes.co.uk/articles/2014/31-january/features/features/time-to-get-serious> (accessed 11 September 2022).
5. William T. Stead, G. Campbell Morgan, Arthur Goodrich and Evan Roberts, *The Welsh Revival & the Story of the Welsh Revival by Eyewitnesses* (Lawton, OK: Trumpet Press, 2015), p. 64.
6. Anne Calver, 'Revival Podcast: What is God Saying and Doing', 14 June 2021: <https://steveuppal.com/revivalpodcast/revivalwhatgodissaying> (accessed 11 September 2022).
7. 'Day of Common Learning 2017: Always Reforming: Reformation', Seattle Pacific Library: <https://spu.libguides.com/DCL2017/Reformation#s-lg-box-wrapper-18675181> (accessed 11 September 2022).
8. 'Kainos', Blue Letter Bible: <https://www.blueletterbible.org/lexicon/g2537/kjv/tr/0-1> (accessed 11 September 2022).
9. C. S. Lewis, *A Grief Observed* (New York, NY: HarperCollins, 2001), p. 66.
10. 'Metanoia', Blue Letter Bible: <https://www.blueletterbible.org/lexicon/g3341/kjv/tr/0-1> (accessed 11 September 2022).
11. R. H. Jarrett and Sumner M. Davenport, *It Works With Simple Keys* (Thousand Oaks, CA: Self-Investment Company, 2007), p. 104.

12. Ed Silvoso, *Strongholds: What they are and how to pull them down* (Bloomington, MN: Chosen Books, 2016), p. 4.

13. Aimee Semple McPherson, *This is That: Personal experiences, sermons and writings of Aimee Semple McPherson* (Eugene, OR: Wipf and Stock Publishers, 2009), p. 677.

14. Leonard Sweet, *Post-Modern Pilgrims: First century passion for the 21st century world* (Nashville, TN: B&H Books, 2000).

15. *Global Christianity: A report on the size and distribution of the world's Christian population* (Washington, DC: Pew Research Center, 2011): <https://www.pewresearch.org/religion/wp-content/uploads/sites/7/2011/12/Christianity-fullreport-web.pdf> (accessed 11 September 2022).

16. Desmond Tutu, '10 Questions for Desmond Tutu', *Time*, 22 March 2010: <http://content.time.com/time/subscriber/article/0,33009,1971410,00.html> (accessed 11 September 2022).

17. Thomas Merton, *Thoughts in Solitude* (London: Burns & Oates, 1997), p. 79.

1 Jesus is Lord

1. N. T. Wright, *For All God's Worth* (London: SPCK Publishing, 1997), p. 1.

2. Michael Frost and Alan Hirsch, *ReJesus: A wild messiah for a missional church* (Ada, MI: Baker Books, 2008), p. 120.

3. S. M. Zwemer, *The Solitary Throne* (London: Pickering and Inglis, 1937), p. 1.

4. A. W. Tozer, *Man: The dwelling place of God* (Camp Hill, PA: Wingspread Publishers, 2008).

5. Lee Camp, *Mere Discipleship: Radical Christianity in a rebellious world* (Grand Rapids, MI: Brazos Press, 2003), p. 28.

6. Andrew Root, *Churches and the Crisis of Decline* (Grand Rapids, MI: Baker Publishing Group, 2022), p. x.

7. 'Christian Ministers and Politics', *The Wells Journal*, 14 December 1911 (British Newspaper Archive), p. 6.

8. Søren Kierkegaard, *Provocations: Spiritual writings of Kierkegaard* (New York, NY: Plough Publishing), p. 227.

9. Jon Tyson and Heather Grizzle, *A Creative Minority: Influencing culture through redemptive participation* (New York, NY: Heather Grizzle Publisher, 2016).

10. Cited in Tyson and Grizzle, *A Creative Minority*, p. 11.

11. Cited by W. K. Lowther Clarke in *The Rule of St Benedict* (London: SPCK, 1931), p. 2.

12. Rod Dreher, *The Benedict Option: A strategy for Christians in a post-Christian nation* (New York, NY: Sentinel, 2017).

13. Alastair MacIntyre, *After Virtue* (Notre Dame, IN: University of Notre Dame Press, 2007), p. 263.

14. Robert Dale, *To Dream Again: How to help your church come alive* (Eugene, OR: Wipf & Stock, 2004), p. 116.

15. Cited by Amy Welborn in 'Suscipe, the Radical Prayer', Ignatian Spirituality: <https://www.ignatianspirituality.com/ignatian-prayer/prayers-by-st-ignatius-and-others/suscipe-the-radical-prayer> (accessed 11 September 2022).

2 Dependent upon the Holy Spirit

1. A. W. Tozer, *Tozer on the Holy Spirit: A 365-day devotional* (Chicago, IN: Moody Publishers, 2015), p. 232.

2. 'Palingenesia', Blue Letter Bible: <https://www.blueletterbible.org/lexicon/g3824/kjv/tr/0-1> (accessed 11 September 2022).

3. Nehemiah Curnock (ed.), *The Journal of the Rev John Wesley*, 24 May 1738 (London: Epworth Press, 1938).

4. Curnock, *Journal of the Rev John Wesley*, 24 May 1738.

5. John Drane, *The McDonaldization of the Church: Spirituality, creativity and the future of the church* (London: Darton, Longman & Todd, 2000).

6. Skye Jethani, 'The Evangelical Industrial Complex & the Rise of Celebrity Pastors (Pt. 1)', *Christianity Today*, 20 February 2012: <https://www.christianitytoday.com/pastors/2012/

february-online-only/evangelical-industrial-complex-rise-of-celebrity-pastors.html> (accessed 15 September 2022).

7. Jackie Pullinger, *Chasing the Dragon* (London: Hodder & Stoughton, 2012), p. 55.

8. Steve Addison, *Movements That Change the World* (Downers Grove, IL: InterVarsity Press, 2009), p. 38.

3 Confident in the gospel

1. 'Dionysius Exiguus', Britannica: <https://www.britannica.com/biography/Dionysius-Exiguus> (accessed 11 September 2022).

2. Melvin Newland, 'Four Jewels of Easter', *Sermon Central*, 23 February 2001: <https://www.sermoncentral.com/sermons/four-jewels-of-easter-melvin-newland-sermon-on-easter-resurrection-34022> (accessed 15 September 2022).

3. 'Euangelion', Blue Letter Bible: <https://www.blueletterbible.org/lexicon/g2098/kjv/tr/0-1> (accessed 11 September 2022).

4. Walter Brueggemann, *Finally Comes the Poet: Daring speech for proclamation* (Minneapolis, MN: Augsburg Fortress Publishers, 1989), p. 1.

5. 'Marks of Mission', Anglican Communion: <https://www.anglicancommunion.org/mission/marks-of-mission.aspx> (accessed 11 September 2022).

6. 'Logos', Blue Letter Bible: <https://www.blueletterbible.org/lexicon/g3056/kjv/tr/0-1> (accessed 11 September 2022).

7. 'Talking Jesus Report 2022', p. 25, Talking Jesus: <https://talkingjesus.org/2022-research> (accessed 15 September 2022).

8. Emma Stark, *The Prophetic Warrior: Operating in your true prophetic authority* (Shippensburg, PA: Destiny Image, 2020), p. 64.

4 A disciple-making community

1. C. S. Lewis, *Mere Christianity* (New York, NY: HarperCollins: 2001), p. 199.

2. Dallas Willard, *The Great Omission: Jesus' essential teachings on discipleship* (London: Monarch Books, 2014).

3. Alan Hirsch and Mark Nelson, *Reframation: Seeing God, people, and mission through reenchanted frames* (Cody, WY: 100 Movements Publishing, 2019), p. 235.

4. Dietrich Bonhoeffer, *The Cost of Discipleship* (London: SCM Press, 2015), p. 44.

5. Walter Bright, 'When he came there was no light, when he left there was no darkness', 7 August 2013: <https://walterbright. net/2013/08/07/when-he-came-there-was-no-light-when-he-left-there-was-no-darkness> (accessed 11 September 2022).

6. 'Baptizō', Blue Letter Bible: <https://www.blueletterbible.org/ lexicon/g907/kjv/tr/0-1> (accessed 11 September 2022).

7. Gary Chapman, *The Five Love Languages: The secret to love that lasts* (Chicago, IN: Moody Publishers, 2009).

8. Bonhoeffer, *Cost of Discipleship*, p. 45.

9. 'Mathētēs', Blue Letter Bible: <https://www.blueletterbible.org/ lexicon/g3101/kjv/tr/0-1> (accessed 11 September 2022).

10. Jon Tyson, *Beautiful Resistance: The joy of conviction in a culture of compromise* (Colorado Springs, CO: Multnomah Press, 2020), p. 3.

11. Dallas Willard, *The Spirit of Disciplines* (London: Hodder & Stoughton, 1996), p. 67.

12. Winfield Bevins, *Marks of a Movement: What the church today can learn from the Wesleyan revival* (Grand Rapids, MI: Zondervan Reflective, 2019), p. 111.

13. 'A covenant with God', The Methodist Church: <https://www. methodist.org.uk/about-us/the-methodist-church/what-is-distinctive-about-methodism/a-covenant-with-god> (accessed 11 September 2022).

5 Churches that plant churches

1. Peter Wagner, *Church Planting for a Greater Harvest* (Eugene, OR: Wipf and Stock Publishers, 1990), p. 11.

2. David Garrison, *Church Planting Movements: How God is redeeming a lost world* (Monument, CO: Wigtake Resources, 2004), p. 189.

3. 'Ekklēsia', Blue Letter Bible: <https://www.blueletterbible.org/lexicon/g1577/kjv/tr/0-1> (accessed 11 September 2022).

4. 'The House of Good', The National Churches Trust: <https://www.houseofgood.nationalchurchestrust.org> (accessed 11 September 2022).

5. Jon Tyson and Heather Grizzle, *A Creative Minority: Influencing culture through redemptive participation* (New York, NY: Heather Grizzle Publisher, 2016), p. 7.

6. Roland Allen, *The Spontaneous Expansion of the Church: And the causes which hinder it* (Cambridge, UK: Lutterworth Press, 2006), p. 185.

7. Lesslie Newbigin, *The Gospel in a Pluralist Society* (Grand Rapids, MI: Eerdmans, 1989), p. 227.

6 A diverse leadership

1. Os Guinness, *The Call: Finding and fulfilling the central purpose of your life* (Nashville, TN: Thomas Nelson, 2003), p. 11.

2. 'Funny Old Game: John Lambie was famed for his quick wit – but which other managers can match him for hilarious quips?', *The Scottish Sun*, 11 April 2018: <https://www.thescottishsun.co.uk/sport/football/2488900/john-lambie-football-manager-quotes> (accessed 11 September 2022).

3. 'Opening of the XV Ordinary General Assembly of the Synod of Bishops', Libreria Editrice Vaticana: <https://www.vatican.va/content/francesco/en/speeches/2018/october/documents/papa-francesco_20181003_apertura-sinodo.html> (accessed 11 September 2022).

4. David Garrison, *Church Planting Movements: How God is redeeming a lost world* (Monument, CO: Wigtake Resources, 2004), p. 189.

5. 'Klēros', Blue Letter Bible: <https://www.blueletterbible.org/lexicon/g2819/kjv/tr/0-1> (accessed 11 September 2022).

6. 'λαϊκός', Wiktionary: <https://en.wiktionary.org/wiki/%CE%BB%CE%B1%CF%8A%CE%BA%CF%8C%CF%82> (accessed 11 September 2022).

7. Cited in J. R. Woodward and Dan White, *The Church as Movement: Starting and sustaining missional-incarnational communities* (London: IVP, 2016), p. 25.

8. Richard Lovelace, *Dynamics of Spiritual Life: An evangelical theology of renewal* (Exeter: Paternoster Press, 1979), p. 207.

9. 'Pray for: Iran', Operation World: <https://operationworld.org/locations/iran> (accessed 11 September 2022).

10. Sarah Zylstra, 'Meet the World's Fastest-Growing Evangelical Movement', *The Gospel Coalition*, 8 February 2021: <https://www.thegospelcoalition.org/article/meet-the-worlds-fastest-growing-evangelical-movement> (accessed 11 September 2022).

11. Darrin J. Rodgers, 'Yoido Full Gospel Church: How women ministers fueled the growth of the world's largest church', *The Flower Pentecostal Heritage Center*, 2 November 2017: <https://ifphc.wordpress.com/2017/11/02/yoido-full-gospel-church-how-women-ministers-fueled-the-growth-of-the-worlds-largest-church> (accessed 11 September 2022).

12. 'The Azusa Street Revival', Apostolic Archives: <https://www.apostolicarchives.com/articles/article/8801925/173190.htm> (accessed 11 September 2022).

13. Winfield Bevins, *Marks of a Movement: What the church today can learn from the Wesleyan revival* (Grand Rapids, MI: Zondervan Reflective, 2019), p. 69.

14. 'Apostolos', Blue Letter Bible: https://www.blueletterbible.org/lexicon/g652/kjv/tr/0-1/ (accessed 11 September 2022).

15. Bevins, *Marks of a Movement*, p. 124.

16. Pete Greig, *The Vision and the Vow* (Brighton: Kingsway Publications, 2005), p. 5.

17. Frances R. Havergal, 'Take My Life and Let It Be', 1874 (public domain).

7 A holy people

1. Jose Luis Gonzalez-Balado, *Mother Teresa: In my own words* (Liguori, MO: Liguori Publications, 1997), p. 5.
2. 'What is the Letter to Diognetus?', Got Questions: <https://www.gotquestions.org/Letter-to-Diognetus.html> (accessed 11 September 2022).
3. 'Hagios', Blue Letter Bible: <https://www.blueletterbible.org/lexicon/g40/kjv/tr/0-1> (accessed 11 September 2022).
4. Cited by Greg Kandra in 'Did the Pope Really Say That?', *Patheos*, 23 July 2013: <https://www.patheos.com/blogs/deaconsbench/2013/07/did-the-pope-really-say-that> (accessed 11 September 2022).
5. Stephanie Dowrick, *Intimacy and Solitude: Balancing closeness and independence* (London: The Women's Press, 2002), p. 215.
6. 'The Welsh Revival – 1904', Revival Library: <https://www.revival-library.org/revival_histories/evangelical/1900/welsh_revival_1904.shtml> (accessed 11 September 2022).
7. Michael Frost and Alan Hirsch, *The Shaping of Things to Come: Innovation and mission for the 21st century church* (Peabody, MA: Hendrickson Publishers, 2003), p. 22.

8 Prioritizing prayer

1. Karl Barth, *The Christian Life: Church dogmatics IV, 4: Lecture fragments* (Grand Rapids, MI: Eerdmans, 1981).
2. 'David Yonggi Cho Sermon: Intercession and Prayer Secrets', YouTube (2015): <https://www.youtube.com/watch?v=vR_x4uHNZpk> (accessed 11 September 2022).
3. 'When the Mountains Flowed Down – Duncan Campbell', Revival Library: <https://www.revival-library.org/revival_histories/evangelical/twentieth_century/hebrides_revival.shtml> (accessed 11 September 2022).

4. Karl Barth, *Church Dogmatics: The doctrine of creation, vol. 3, part 3* (London: T & T Clark International, 2000), p. 288.

5. C. S. Lewis, *The Screwtape Letters* (New York, NY: HarperCollins, 2002), p. 2.

6. Steve Addison, *Movements That Changed the World* (Downers Grove, IL: InterVarsity Press, 2009).

7. Translation by Ludwig Bieler, cited in 'The Confession of St. Patrick', Island Guide: <https://www.islandguide.co.uk/history/patrick.htm> (accessed 19 September 2022).

8. J. C. Ryle, *Holiness*, 5th edn (Hope Mills, NC: Heritage Bible Fellowship, 2011), p. 40.

9. 'SS *Canberra*', Wikipedia: <https://en.wikipedia.org/wiki/SS_Canberra> (accessed 11 September 2022).

10. Andrew Root, *Churches and the Crisis of Decline* (Grand Rapids, MI: Baker Publishing Group, 2022), p. 143.

11. '*Saint Patrick's Breastplate*', Wikipedia: <https://en.wikipedia.org/wiki/Saint_Patrick%27s_Breastplate> (accessed 11 September 2022).

Conclusion

1. Oswald Chambers, *My Utmost for His Highest* (Grand Rapids, MI: Our Daily Bread Publishing, 2017), p. 137.

2. 'Jean Darnell's Vision', Call The Nation To Prayer: <https://ctntp.uk/background/jean-darnalls-vision> (accessed 11 September 2022).

3. Richard Baxter, *The Saints' Everlasting Rest: The practical works of Richard Baxter, 3* (Grand Rapids, MI: Soli Deo Gloria, 2000).

4. Cited in Mark Sayers, *Reappearing Church: The hope for renewal in the rise of our post-Christian culture* (Chicago, IN: Moody Publishers, 2019), p. 162.

5. Arthur Wallis, *In the Day of Thy Power: The scriptural principles of revival* (Fort Washington, PA: Click Publications, 2010), p. 202.

6. William Faulkner, cited in Sam di Bonaventura's program notes to Elie Siegmeister's *Symphony no. 5*, Baltimore Symphony Concert (5 May 1977).